Pocket

GUIDE

for

DANCERS

Taira Foo

ISBN 978-1-54391-580-8

Dedicated to all those who chose to follow their dreams.

Contents

Prologue

So you've done your training, now what?

After relentless hours of training, encouragement from your teachers perfecting your technique and showcasing your skills at your graduation, you've demonstrated how far you've come, and how all the tears and pain were worth it to become a dancer. And, as you pause to take it all in, do you know where you are headed next?

The journey to carving a career in the dance/performance industry comes with many curve balls. Having witnessed a lot of dancers giving up on their dreams as they faced rejection, one audition after the other, I knew I had to do something. This pocket guide is the result. Within it are nuggets of inspiration and pieces of my life to guide you to a successful dancing career.

The dance world has dark corners, hard to navigate on a winter night, and can often feel overwhelmingly lonely. But, don't despair - I've been there and would like to reassure you that if you just focus on your goals and match them with the right actions, you will get where you need to be.

This pocket guide will help you to affirm why you started dancing in the first place and will inspire you to push harder and to never give up easily on your chosen path.

Writing a book was a goal of mine. Even though I've never written one before, I persevered and believed that I could put it together and help many fellow dancers in the process and, here we are.

I wrote this pocket guide as a reference to be kept by your side along your journey. It never ages and, as your journey flows, I hope it will help you measure how far you've come and where you need to head next.

• •

ACKNOWLEDGMENTS

I would like to thank Charlotte Ketteridge for her beautiful book cover design and Rebecca Sachdev for the awesome layout and design. Grace Kadzere, Della Van Baars, Aidan Pasquale and Clive Ketteridge, thank you for all your help.

Alan Walker, Garry Lake and Rolfe Klement, thank you for the use of your wonderful images. Thank you to Bradley Salter, Joshua Rees Ivey, Lewis Haywood, Fenia Tsikitikou and Elena Tsikitikou for being part of those images.

Thank you to Debbie o' Brien, Irene Cotton CDG, Sammi Lee Jayne and Joshua Rees Ivey for your words of wisdom and special mention to Eve Leveaux - if it wasn't for you, I would not be writing this book.

And, finally, thank you to my wonderful family and friends for your continued love and support.

"The big secret in life is that there is no big secret. Whatever your goal, you can get there if you're willing to work," Oprah Winfrey.

My Story

How It All Started

I was a late starter when it came to dance. Whilst a lot of people have the opportunity to start as early as the age of five, my feet only started moving rhythmically at seventeen. I was brought up in Derby and my family was in neither theatre, nor were they exposed to it in any way. The only dance I can recall was the little I saw on television, on Top of the Pops.

I had absolutely no clue about how to be a dancer and that it could be a career. In secondary school, if you were asked what you wanted to do after school and you happened to mention dance, you would be automatically pushed towards the P.E. teacher and, in so doing, the system confirmed that to be a dancer was a fruitless dream. In my mind, I thought dance careers didn't exist. Can you imagine the number of people who had the potential to dance, but missed their chance because of this? Quite a few, I think.

However, those notions were soon to be dispelled from my life by a lady who visited our secondary school. She specialised in community dance and I shall forever remain grateful for her instinct to see that which others couldn't. She thought I could do well within the performance industry and introduced me to a wonderful dance teacher, Eve Leveaux. And so my journey began.

I remember certain moments very vividly - like during one of my Saturday ballet classes with a group of kids a decade younger than me, when one little girl said, "we have a really old girl in our class. She is seventeen!"

I also met a girl called Nicky Davis who seemed to be at practice all day and upon asking her why so much time, she mentioned she was training full time to be a dancer. Shocked and almost falling off my chair, I realised for the first time in my life that one could become a professional dancer. What an exciting light bulb moment it was for me!

After my talk with her, I spoke with the school principal to see if this was something I stood a chance at. Whilst I knew very little, no fear could hold me back from sharing what I wanted. As I spoke with Eve she almost choked, and at the same time spat her tea out, when she heard me say I wanted to be a professional ballerina. What she couldn't ignore, though, was the passion and the enthusiasm I was exuding. So, she took me under her wing and on a scholarship; she would go on to empower me with most of my dance skills. And the rest, as the saying goes, became history.

After a year of training, I started auditioning for the bigger dance colleges in London. Whilst I got accepted into all of them, I ended up with a conservatoire that offered me a part scholarship. On top of heavily stretching my parents' purse strings, I found the conservatoire quite restricting. It limited my dance creativity and so I made the decision to go back home, to Derby. For two years I trained mostly in ballet, to give myself a solid foundation for the other dance styles I liked. I travelled up and down to London on a coach that left as early as five in the morning to expose myself to other styles of dance, including jazz and commercial jazz. All the travel never bothered me because I loved it and knew without a single doubt that this was the only path for me. I was like a racehorse with blinkers on - nothing could have persuaded me to pursue a different career. I had tunnel vision. Knowing that I could actually do this for a living gave me fire in my belly and a vision I just had to fulfill.

Whilst I mainly trained in ballet, today I specialise in contemporary and hip-hop dance. All in all, it took me three years of training before my first job came knocking.

My first audition was touch and go. Seriously. I auditioned and immediately got cut. Feeling sick to my stomach and wondering why I hadn't made it, I chose to go and do a class at the ever-famous Pineapple Dance Studios, as opposed to dwelling on the rejection. It was here that I was spotted by a choreographer and, before I knew it, I had secured my first professional job. It was fantastic!

The love and clarity I had for dance would later propel me to consider musical theatre and, yes, I had never learnt to sing. I wanted to be in the West End and the first way to eventually, or perhaps hopefully, get there was to start the same way as most people – hello, singing in the shower and karaoke weekends! Equating dance muscles to music, I knew that the more I trained my voice, the closer I would be to eventually pulling off a song decently.

Believing in myself beyond anything, anyone and the reality that my voice was not a typical standard musical theatre voice played a major part in driving away any fears. I exposed myself to open auditions. Why open auditions? Because I had no agent at the time, so they were the only ones I could attend. The advantage for me was the amount of valuable information about the industry I extracted and learnt from these open auditions.

The hard work paid off when I got to sing in my first West End show and it was for an original cast! If I tell you that beyond self–belief, I know exactly how I got selected, I would be lying. I don't know or remember how I got through those auditions. And, surprisingly, when that contract ended, the MD complimented me on my singing journey and reminded me to keep going.

• • • • • • • • • • • • •

LEARNING ON THE JOB

I literally learnt everything on the job. Being a late starter there was only so much I could learn within that short amount of time. Everything was learnt by a nod of the head at the right times and looking like I understood everything that was being directed or spoken.

When I got my first West End show I spent the first week miming, as I didn't know what a harmony was, let alone harmony lines. I mean when I look back now it seems crazy that there was so much that I didn't know, yet I had this total belief in myself and my abilities. Had I been aware of the unknown, I am not sure how confident I would have gone into that rehearsal. In the end, I think it was better that I was naive to the situation.

For the first rehearsal of the show, I remember getting fully dressed into my fiercest dance combo - which was my hair up, dance trainers on - and BAM I was ready to go into rehearsals! When I turned up, I noticed that there weren't many people dressed for a full on dance rehearsal. Where were the leg warmers? The buns? The tight leggings? It looked like everyone had his or her best gear on instead!

As more of the cast came in, I started to feel a little out of place and a bit foolish. When everyone got there we were given coffee, tea and croissants. Meanwhile, I was thinking, *"oh my goodness, where's the hardcore warm up? This is like a get together not a gruelling rehearsal."* We all sat down in a circle after everyone had said their hellos and had their tea and coffee. We were going to do a read through. *"A read through? What's that?"* Of course, I sort of understood, but I just didn't know this is what happened. After we had read through Act One we had another break!!!

Some of the cast sang their songs and I remember very clearly the goose pimples I had on my arms as they sang. It was so amazing! I felt like I was in my own dreamland, the talent I was surrounded by was absolutely incredible and I was part of it! Me! It was the best feeling in the world!

In the afternoon we started learning songs. Everyone started to pull out their recording devices. I didn't have anything to record the harmonies on; I didn't know we had to. Yes, I was the only one who didn't have one. Back then we used Dictaphones. So, on my second day of rehearsal, before we started, I waited for an hour outside an electrical shop for them to open and I bought myself a Dictaphone. *"There you go, all done and no one noticed!"* I remember telling my mom and dad, "we are learning harmonies and I don't know what they are." And clearly neither did they!

On the same day, we were asked what our vocal ranges were. As you've probably guessed by now, I didn't know what mine was. *"Do I join the alto group or soprano? What is an alto?"* I knew I could sing high and low, I could actually do both, but was asked to join the alto group. We were also learning 6-part harmonies! Talk about being thrown into the deep end. But, not to worry, I was well-equipped with snorkels and goggles in the shape of determination and faith. I had a lot of gumption! Luckily, I learnt how to sing in this show. It was a training journey all by itself and I was getting paid to do it while living my dream of being on a West End stage! Brilliant!!!

When I worked on a cruise ship, I was told we were blocking the next day and in my head, I was thinking, *"OK, what the hell is that?"* I literally didn't know, but soon understood what it was.

Stage Left and Stage Right are the simplest things I didn't know. When I performed in a Christmas show I was asked to move to Stage Right, so I confidently moved to Stage Left, only to be told that that was the wrong way. Oh God, the looks on my cast members' faces were priceless!

I remember the first time I was given a dresser. A dresser was someone to dress me. Well, I can dress myself, so this was really nice. And she helped with the changes too!!!

It's okay to not know things as long as you find out what you need to know and you stay calm about the fact that you were unaware of some vital things in the industry. It's a lot of fun finding out.

When I first started auditioning, I was asked to deliver a monologue and I didn't really know what this was as I had never performed one before. It was for a big show at The National and the audition was with a very well-known director. A few days before the audition I got a call from my agent to say they wanted to see me. They wanted to know what I was going to do for the monologue. "*I know!*" I thought to myself, "*I will write one.*" I wrote my own monologue based on my own circumstances, as I knew little about acting, but thought I would be able to connect with something I had written from experience - and I think I was right.

On the day of the audition, I walked into a fairly large-sized black room where I was met by the presence of two very established people in the industry. I felt very small and a total fake. There was the director looking straight at me, holding out his hand and introducing himself and I just looked at him in admiration and hoped I wasn't going to embarrass myself with my self-written monologue that I had only written a couple of days before. He went on to introduce me to the pianist who seemed really lovely and I was immediately put at ease by his warm smile.

I began my monologue sitting on a chair and, as I started to talk, everything else in the room seemed to disappear. I couldn't really see the other two people in the room as I just zoned out into my own space. Delivering that monologue, I was filled with total belief and confidence in what I was doing and it felt amazing. "That's great", he said and asked me to do it again, but differently. So I did. He then asked me to sing, so I did. He asked me why I didn't sing more. I didn't really know what to say to this but took it as a compliment. The whole experience was an enjoyable one. I left the room feeling a lot more confident than I had done when I walked in and I felt valued and deserving of being in that audition room and the industry.

Even though I didn't get the job, I learned a lot from the experience. Mainly, that I was totally capable of doing well in this industry and with a bit of determination and will power, I would make it. They did, however, ring my agent to say they really liked me, but not that time around and they didn't even have to do that.

I could have taken the fact that I had never done a monologue before and used it as an excuse not to try or maybe not even go to the audition. But, where else was I going to get the information and experience I needed if I didn't go? We didn't have Google or YouTube, so there was limited information on things like monologues, auditions, etc. To find out what was expected, I had to try via the auditions. I could have talked myself out of this audition, but instead, I made the decision not to.

I only ever trained in ballet. We used to have a jazz teacher come in a couple of times. In essence, I didn't really have the training. I went to London numerous times to take classes there, but not as much as I wanted as I didn't have the funds to do so. In the end, I didn't have a consistent training in jazz.

I auditioned for a dance company called Jazzexchange, which still exists now. I got the job and so began my Jazz training and I loved it. We were learning a new show and had company class every morning before going into rehearsals. Being taught by the amazing Sheron Wray and learning from the surrounding dancers, who had all trained at prestigious colleges, I was like a sponge and I just loved the genre. Sheron was a great inspiration and taught me many things. I was also exposed to improvisation for the first time and yes, we came up with our own ways to improvise within the show, which was performed at The Royal Opera House. I loved every second of this contract; it was wonderful; I learnt so much from the choreographer and the other dancers.

I would suggest always going to the audition because you never know what will come out of it and you will always learn something if you go with the right mindset. Never block your path with things you can overcome. Just make sure you do the necessary preparation and research before you go to the audition, even if it is a couple of days before.

. . . .

The Highlights and The Present

One of my career highlights has to be recording at Abbey Road Studios. What an experience! As we recorded an album for a new show, we saw the faces of an iconic band behind the glass and each one of us in that room felt like something wonderful was happening. The energy in the room was incredible and each of us just wanted that moment to last forever.

Ringing my mum just before I went on stage for a live performance at Buckingham Palace for the Queen's Jubilee was surreal! It made me feel very happy to share the experience with my parents, after all the years of support. It was the moment I got to say "Thank You" for believing in me.

Another highlight was Party at The Park. It was a reminder of what absolute bliss lies within this industry if you are willing to not give up. Dancing for the Queen (again) next to a well-known boxer and rubbing shoulders with some truly awesome people, famous and non-famous, was incredible. Future jobs would later follow, all very different and amazing in their own ways.

I now choreograph and teach. I moved on to a new passion and never thought it would fulfil me as much as it has. To create, makes me feel like I danced my best dance or sang my best song - the feelings are the same. I have choreographed many pantomimes, shows for universities and colleges, music videos, and a couple of short films. Working as a teacher has also given me many rewards, including seeing many of my students succeed in the industry. I love seeing confidence grow in young people, whether they choose a dance career or not.

Another goal of mine was to set up my own dance company. Setting up my own dance company filled me with fear, but it has now become one of the best decisions I ever made. This was the beginning of a new adventure and I am still on this journey. I was awarded funding last year from the Arts Council and I created a piece of work that will stay with me forever. It was successful because it has developed me as an artist and allowed me to have an outlet for my creativity. Heeding my own advice, I am taking the time to look at how grateful I am for the things around me and I am allowing myself to enjoy this path while working towards growing as a choreographer.

I have now been dancing for 23 years of my life and I am still going. For those people that may say your chosen path is short-lived, I would like to tell you, having just had my 40th birthday, that I have no plans to stop anytime soon. Choosing a dance career is almost like starting a business - no one but you needs to believe it can be done. Most say it can't be done and others will say it's too difficult. But, if you have that feeling of a racehorse with blinkers on, no one will be able to stop you.

Statistically, the dance industry is often frowned upon for having too many participants in it, yet little money. If my experience is anything to go by, this is an industry filled with opportunities. Opportunities to be a lot of characters at different stages, meet new people, travel the world and live your vision. There's room for everyone and, if I could do it, so can you!

Considering the hard times and the time it took to build my career, would I do it all again if given the chance? Absolutely! What would change? Not much; however, in hindsight, I would appreciate what I had more and take more time to be grateful for things outside of dance. I rarely went on holiday as I didn't want to miss out on an audition, and I love to travel. I guess I got to see the oceans dancing on a cruise ship, and if I had done everything by the book, then you probably wouldn't be reading this now.

My biggest piece of advice would be to enjoy the journey!!!

By choosing to read this pocket guide, I know that you want to learn. I believe you are on the right track. By being observant and absorbing as much as I could I became a better dancer and got more opportunities. Being observant and hungry to learn is far more valuable than being envious of the girl in bright green tights.

"Whether you think you can or think you can't. You are right," Henry Ford.

Photographer: Garry Lake

Chapter 1

Facing the Real World

Getting into the industry and showcasing your art is both exciting and overwhelming. I believe that starting on the right foot is imperative. And, as Martha Graham says, "Dance is communication, and so the great challenge is to speak clearly, beautifully and with inevitability." This chapter is to help you start communicating your art with a sense of direction.

Grab your notebook, mobile, or tablet (whichever you are comfortable writing notes on) and let's get going. But let's begin by reflecting on you - the "you" that the outside world doesn't know. Let's do this in three steps:

First, at the top of a blank page, or below, answer the question of **WHY DANCE?**

Write as many answers as you can, everything that comes to you. If you are struggling to be honest with that, try adding to this section answers to questions such as:

1. Why did you choose this career? OR
2. Do you get excited and stay enthusiastic about embarking on a professional dance career?

_____

_____

_____

_____

_____

_____

_____

_____

_____

_____

_____

Look at all the answers, summarise them and create an acronym that means something to you. For example, if your answers included bringing happiness to other people, story telling through dance, because you love it and it gives you a reason to feel alive daily, your acronym could be **LASH** (Love, Alive, Storytelling and Happiness). Anything that works as a good reminder for you, really.

Secondly, on the next page, or below, ask yourself **WHAT IF I WERE TO FAIL** as a professional dancer? The answers you put down, or can think of, determine if being a dancer is what you really want. The answers can also feed into whether you would lose all the answers to the first part of this exercise.

1. What would be the consequences if you failed as a dancer?
2. What would you do instead and would you be happy?

_____

_____

_____

_____

_____

_____

_____

_____

_____

Your answers, as you read them, will confirm how important dance is to you and help you unleash motivation from within. Sometimes it helps to see the negatives next to the positives to comprehend how badly you want something and all that's at stake.

This is, by no means, to say that you are going to fail; it's simply to remind you that, unless you put your all in, success will be hard to attain. Keep in mind that these exercises are just a guide to help you, based on my experiences in the industry.

Lastly answer the questions, **WHAT IF I SUCCEED** as a professional dancer?

1. What would it feel like?
2. Who would you celebrate with?
3. What does that success look like?

Remember that feeling and come back to it when you feel out of touch with your path.

_____

_____

_____

_____

_____

_____

Because there are different definitions of success in one's life, we will look at goals shortly, as they are the common metric of success for most people in the world.

It's so easy to get lost, therefore, a repetition of the above exercise assists you with re-evaluating why you chose to dance and how to get focused again, remembering NEVER TO QUIT!

• • • • • • • • • • • • •

GOALS

Going from one audition to another? Let's get more clarity on what we are trying to achieve. You need goals, even if they seem too bold because you are just starting out. Just remember to have faith in yourself and believe you can make it. If other dancers that came before you could do it, what's stopping you?

On a blank page, or below, start writing your career goals. Writing down your goals serves as a reminder of what you are working towards.

_____

_____

_____

_____

_____

_____

_____

_____

_____

The best goals are SMART ones. This means that they need to be Specific, Measurable, Achievable, Realistic and Time-based. This will allow you to track them easily. For example, if you would like to be in a musical in a year, your timeline is a year to work on your voice, getting to know where to audition, and trying again and again until you make it.

Because the brain connects better with images, how about you save these goals as images and put them on a vision board, so you can see them every morning when you wake up and every night before you go to bed? Something happens in the subconscious when you keep seeing your future right in front of you every single day. This is where actions to match that future tend to kick in.

. . . .

Goal Actioning

It's good and honourable to have dreams translated into goals. But, that's all they are until we start translating them into daily actions, no matter how small.

Below, or on a blank page, let's write down the actions that we have to take to meet these goals. It could be the number of auditions you promise yourself to attend on a weekly basis, despite how your body feels. It could also be the people that you need to make contact with to secure certain opportunities; the further training you need to receive; the hours spent practising daily; the number of workshops to attend; the writing to casting directors... Capture it all.

I've filled in the first one as a guide.

GOAL - Grow my dance network.
ACTION – Introduce myself to at least one person at every audition or class that I take. **Now you continue:**

_____

_____

_____

_____

_____

_____

_____

_____

_____

_____

_____

_____

_____

_____

_____

_____

Even if all you have is one goal, that's great. This is your journey and no one else's. You have to do it your own way.

· ·

"I am committed to my art. I believe that all art has its ultimate goal, the union between the material, the human and the divine. I believe that to be the reason for the very existence of art," Michael Jackson.

REMEMBER!

- Know your authentic self to avoid getting lost in your career journey.
- Write down your goals as a career map to your dreams.
- Visualise and believe that you are no different from iconic dancers; you can achieve the same success.
- Consistent actions, daily, are how goals are achieved.

KNOWLEDGE IS POWER!**

Keep learning and empowering yourself through platforms such as:

- http://jamesclear.com/
- http://www.success.com/

And, if you can find the time, it wouldn't hurt to read the following book:

- *Leading An Inspired Life* by Jim Rohn.

** Website links were last checked in January 2017.

Photographer: Alan Walker

Chapter 2

Building Your Image

You've dug deep internally and know that to dance is your present and future, what follows? The industry is yet to see your work - they don't know who you are. You want them to know you, so you stand out. Creating and building your image becomes an important part of this industry.

Building your image is branding yourself to be more marketable. Your image is there to help you get better job opportunities. The more people are impressed by you and want to see you, the higher your chances with choreographers, directors and casting directors. A good "Image" also creates a platform for you to connect with better contacts and heighten your industry recognition levels.

When you become a professional dancer, getting paid for it matters and that's why your image needs to be commercially appealing and memorable. Whilst it might sound daunting, with a bit of hard work, and most importantly authenticity, you will be able to build your image easily.

What are the different elements that will bring your image together? Simplified and summarised, the powerful visual elements of your image/brand will include:

i.   Photographs
ii.   What you wear
iii. Portfolio/CV

iv. Showreel

v. The Digital World (Website and social media - covered in the next chapter).

An ex–student of mine, Sammi Lee Jayne, who went on to dance with Rita Ora, Rihanna, Robbie Williams, and on X Factor, says that when she became a professional dancer it took her a while to learn the commercial industry and the image she needed to portray to match who she is and her skills. "Image is important. I went through most hair colours and styles, as I tried to discover my personal image. However, with consistent training, taking the right classes and by being true to myself, I eventually got there," she commented. "Beyond great photos, you have to believe in yourself, first and foremost; get seen and work hard".

Eventually, as dancers, we will get there with the image of who we are, which in essence makes our personal brands.

. . . .

PHOTOGRAPHS

Remember the idiom, "*a picture tells a thousand words,*" a picture definitely does. Photos are the reason why social media platforms that have images at their core, like Instagram and Pinterest, are doing so well. Great photos tell the person looking at them that you made an effort and are serious about your career. Sloppy pictures tend to turn off directors or choreographers. As a choreographer, I've come across photos that resulted in me completely ignoring the dancer's CV. I would rather that didn't happen to you.

Great images have the power to evoke emotions and stay in people's minds for a long time and, in some instances, forever. You are not a photographer, so this will be hard to execute by yourself. But, you can still have fun practising. I would suggest that you consider spending a few pennies by hiring a photographer. Just keep in mind that this is an investment into your future and it will pay off one day. It's imperative that you look at the photographer's profile and see if it matches your style, budget and the holistic image you want to portray.

There is a range of good photographers in the country including:

- Garry Lake
  http://garrylakephotography.tumblr.com

- Rolfe Klement
  http://www.creativesunshine.com

- Alan Walker
  http://alan752.wixsite.com/aw-imagez

- Nicola Selby
  http://nicolaselby.com

- Martin Bell
  http://www.martinbell-photography.co.uk/dance-and-theatre

- Laurent Liotardo
  http://www.laurentliotardophotography.com
- Paul Colwell
  http://www.dancephotographer.co.uk
- David White
  http://www.dancephotography.co.uk

Remember the above are only a guide. Go onto the London Dance website (http://londondance.com/directory/dance-resources/photographers/), as they have more than 50 listed photographers to choose from.

Your photos are going to be on your CV/ portfolio, website and social media pages, so I would recommend that you use a pro to get the right images. You need to make sure that the photographs look like you. When I have gone through a selection process, some performers look totally different from their photographs; it is important that it is YOU the casting directors see.

. . . .

What To Wear

Whilst I've emphasised photos for all that encompasses you on paper, your image away from that, and in front of your audience, matters too. This business is very small and there will always be someone who knows you. Make sure you are painting a good picture of yourself - work hard, stay humble, and focused.

Get your look right for the right audition (please refer to the relevant audition wear in Chapter 5). When I first started out, I had little knowledge about image. I didn't know how to dress for an audition and didn't understand that you needed to wear different clothes for different auditions. So, when I first began auditioning, it was hair in a bun, black tights and black leotard, not much make-up *et voila*, I was done! I went for many auditions dressed like this - mostly musical theatre auditions. I was lost in a crowd of brightly coloured clothes worn by other dancers that had their hair styled and made a serious effort to put their make-up on. The only musical I was suitable for in these clothes was Cats and Chicago.

Another good example was when I was auditioning for a big show. The first time I auditioned for this, I wore my hair slick back in a bun and, again, wore black tights and leotard, just as I mentioned above. The panel didn't even look at me. The movement was very grounded and almost reflected street dance in the 90s, so the clothes I was wearing didn't compliment the movement and, once again, I was lost in a sea of brightly coloured individuals. However, the second time around I decided to wear brightly coloured clothes, took my hair out of the bun and danced exactly the same as the first time. I got the job! There was absolutely nothing different about the way I performed the audition, but most importantly perhaps what my look portrayed.

. . . .

CV/ PORTFOLIO

A great CV does not take its intended reader on a meandering long journey before they can find out what your dance skills or specialities are. Forget long CVs and say hello to a punchy and short CV with a headshot image that pulls the reader in. You know how vanity is considered a sin, when it comes to your CV, embrace vanity. Get your face into the reader's face, literally!

Keep in mind that your CV doesn't have to be a duplication of what you put on your website about yourself. The website section, which we will discuss in the next chapter, allows you more freedom to tell your story. Your CV, however, is very important in that it covers the small, but important, details such as your height, that choreographers/ directors need. If you can't put your CV together, seek help, unless you've already bagged yourself an agent to represent you, as they will then help you with that.

The following is an example of what a CV should showcase. You can use it as a guide:

Insert your full name here (preferably in a large font)

Insert your contact details here (Address, telephone number, email address and if you have an agent representing you, include them here).

Insert a shoulder image here (show your face clearly)

Height: XXX

Playing Age: XX – YY

Eye Colour: XXX

Hair Colour: XXX

Hair Length: XXX

Voice: XXX

Training

(List the training you've been certified in and the respective dance colleges)

Credits to date

(List all credits starting with the most recent; keep this clear, simple and honest)

Television Credits

(If you have these, list them here)

Special Dance Skills

(list the different genres of dance that you excel at)

Other Skills

(If you have other skills such as roller-skating , gymnastics, aerial or circus work, put them here)

You might also want to include links to videos on your YouTube channel or your website. They can range from past performances whilst you were training, to routines at which you excel, to professionally shot ones, budget allowing of course.

In the event that you would rather go with an agent from the word go, have a feel for them and choose wisely before you tie down a few years of your career to a representative that might not deliver what you need.

There is a list of agents in the book in Chapter 4. You will find out about other agents if you are in touch with the dance scene and make sure you don't miss out on word of mouth.

Remember to pay attention to every detail in your CV. Grammatical errors and typos come across as unprofessional. Erica Jong said it better, "I think professionalism is important, and professionalism means you get paid."

. . . .

SHOWREEL

I definitely consider a showreel as an audition that you have control over. If you don't make an audition, your showreel could be what gets you called in for an in-person audition. You, therefore, need to make it great.

Because casting directors don't always have the whole day to watch through each showreel in full, I would suggest that your best material is at the beginning of the showreel. That way, if the panel doesn't finish watching it, they would have at least caught a glimpse of who you are as a dancer.

Keeping it short, two to three minutes long, and interesting also improves the chances of potential employers watching it in full. Don't be scared to use music that showcases your talent differently to what every dancer might be doing. It's important, however, to make sure that your music flows well. If you are good at more than one dance genre, the music should transition well to showcase that as well.

In the absence of a budget, a showreel is something you can put together with the help of your friends or family.

All smartphones have made it easier for you to record your videos without having to hire a professional. Whatever you choose to put up, if you don't have the time to scour through YouTube for content on how to edit videos, there are plenty platforms where you can edit your videos:

- http://www.apple.com/imovie/ (This software comes standard with all the Apple computers, tablets and phones)
- http://www.windows-movie-maker.org (Helps if you are not on an Apple product)
- http://fixounet.free.fr/avidemux/
- http://www.ffmpeg.org
- https://www.blender.org
- https://www.cnet.com
- https://www.lwks.com

With a showreel, make sure the people who will watch it can see YOU. Once, on a show I worked on, we had a girl drop out and we needed to replace her urgently, so we had to go with recommendations. We went through the selection process by making use of showreels and there was one girl that I personally thought would have done a great job, but, sadly, her showreel let her down.

• •

"If your words or images are not on point, making them dance in colour won't make them relevant," Edward Tufte.

REMEMBER!

- Branding yourself is exciting, as long as you stay true to whom you are.
- Your image is everything and, with hard work, humility, and focus, you will enjoy sharing it with the world.
- Attention to detail in your CV/ Portfolio is very important.
- Have fun making your showreel and keep it interesting to its viewers.

KNOWLEDGE IS POWER!**

Keep learning and empowering yourself through platforms such as:

- http://www.bigbrandsystem.com
- https://blog.hubspot.com/marketing
- https://brandyourself.com
- http://www.ted.com

And if you can find the time, it wouldn't hurt to read the following books:

- The Power of Visual Storytelling: How to use Visuals, Videos…by Ekaterina Walter and Jessica Gioglio.
- *Onward* by Howard Schultz.

**Website links were last checked in January 2017.

Photographer: Rolfe Klement

Chapter 3

Taking Your Career Online

If there's one thing that the online world has done for the dance industry, it is that now we all have almost the same opportunities to showcasing our talents. Most people have smartphones these days, which means they can access content online from anywhere and at any given time.

By embracing the digital/ online world, you can showcase your dance skills at minimal costs, but just your time.

- - - - - - - - - - - - -

WEBSITE

A website is a good place to have links to your performances, CV and contact details in one place. Done correctly, it is the best marketing arsenal you could ever have. This is where choreographers, directors, and people, in general, can see what you are about. It needs to be clean and accessible. Make sure there's not too much information on there and keep it simple. You could use my website as an example, www.tairafoo.com.

Your website will make it easier for potential future employers to get in touch with you directly, especially if you don't have an agent.

If you want people to keep coming back to your website, then make it look simple and have more visuals. Take care to not make them too large that they take forever to download, or make them too small that the quality looks poor. Every time you post new content, remember to share it on your social media platforms. It's all so exciting that eventually, the more you do this, the higher the chances of it becoming your second nature.

If you don't have the budget, then you could learn how to put together a website yourself. Among many others, platforms where you could do that include *but aren't limited* to:

- http://www.wix.com
- https://www.sitebuilder.com
- https://www.websitebuilder.com

. . . .

Social Media

When I click on personal videos dancers have taken during class and rehearsal, it actually shows how many people have seen their video. I am taken back by the number of people that look at their posts! We are talking hundreds and thousands!

There are more than 1 billion people on social media globally. It's free and presents a lot of opportunities. The different platforms allow you to build your portfolio at your own pace. As a choreographer, I have often looked at auditionees' Facebook pages

- mainly if I have been undecided about people - to see if they have any further footage of their work, etc.

Because there are so many platforms to choose from, it's best to decide on which ones you are going to invest more time on, to market your expertise. For example, if you choose to use Facebook, Twitter, Instagram, SnapChat, LinkedIn, Pinterest and YouTube all at the same time, can you manage all those platforms at once? Or would you rather use your time and efforts where you are likely to benefit more? Will you be able to keep them updated regularly, so you don't lose followers? Or, perhaps, try them all and then stick with those that excite you the most.

Let's take a look at these platforms, keeping in mind that your style of posts/updates/content will be consistent with you. It's up to you what you post. Have fun until you start getting some traction.

Facebook

You probably have your own personal page. Do you want to expose your dance career there, too? Remember that your friends and family are likely to tag you in pictures that say a lot about your life outside of dance.

My recommendation would be that you keep everything positive. It's always good to have a separate page for your dance career, and it's also free, so why not? You can upload a lot of class videos, rehearsals or whatever you like onto your business/dance career page.

I use both of my pages; I upload on my personal page more than my other, as I guess more people will see it and it's the one I automatically go to. Both work; I think your business page, however, allows you to upload more frequently about your career.

Instagram

Again, I recommend a separate page if you are a dancer who likes to post a lot about your personal life. Make your page a "Public Figure" one so that you can put up contact details easily.

Instagram is cool, simple and is used by a lot of artists in the industry. I would say this is the most used by dancers and choreographers that want to showcase their work.

SnapChat

This platform's videos and pictures last for twenty-four hours and then they automatically delete. I personally think that if you have the time to invest in it, you can have fun here. Statistically, though, as of December 2016, most of its users are teenagers. Again, if you like it, go for it.

Pinterest

Yes, it's very visual, like Instagram. However, of all social media platforms, it has way too many images, and works more for inspiration. Share what you like, but it still has to improve on how dancers can use it to market themselves.

LinkedIn

Because of how professional it is, having a profile here may connect you to choreographers and directors. I, personally, feel that it requires more time and thought about what you share or which conversations you engage in. Having it as another online CV, in the beginning, is great. You can always re-look at participating a bit more once you have a better sense of where your career is headed. I haven't seen any audition listings here, but who knows, that might change in the future.

Twitter

Real-time engagement and a great place to pick up what's happening in the industry by following dance/performance critics, directors, choreographers, companies you like and many dance organisations. By including visuals when you post, you will get more responses, either as likes, retweets, etc. And you also get free analytics on the people engaging with your content.

YouTube

Because right now you probably don't have the budget for a website with huge bandwidth, YouTube should be your friend. You can easily post and host videos here that you can share on your website and your social media platforms without slowing down your website's downloading speed.

As you start to understand what most interests your target audiences, you can also start adding bits and pieces of yourself, aligned to what they like and appreciate about you. It's also easy to set up and only requires you to register with a Gmail account.

Whichever platforms you end up choosing always remember:

- You are not going to get hundreds of followers or fans in a month. Directors aren't going to find or contact you immediately either.
- You cannot be on social media all day. Commit to times when you will check up on it. Could be once, twice or thrice a day - first thing in the morning, during a lunch break or in the evening - whatever works for you. Be careful, as you probably already know, it can become addictive.
- Use popular hashtags relevant to your content and not because they are sensational.
- Try to stay away from social media when consuming alcohol. Mistakes can happen. No one wants the message

to your partner as a tweet. These things happen to the best of us.

· ·

"There are a lot of pros and cons about social media; it's just how you choose to handle it and how you have to be prepared for the negatives as well," Aubrey Peeples.

REMEMBER!

- Keep learning. Social media has become the equaliser between those that have and those that don't. Even with a zero budget, you can make it work for you.
- Make sure to have your showreels prepared - you never know who you might bump into.

KNOWLEDGE IS POWER!**

Keep learning and empowering yourself through platforms such as:

- http://www.danceinforma.com
- http://www.socialmediaexaminer.com/getting-started/

And if you can find the time, it wouldn't hurt to read the following book:

- Self-Marketing Power: Branding Yourself As a Business of One by Jeff Beals

**Website links last checked in January 2017.

Photographer: Rolfe Klement

Chapter 4

Making
Connections

We have all heard people say it's all about who you know. I believe, to an extent, this is true and making connections can only add positively to reaching your goals.

Making connections is a way forward - getting your name out there and your face seen. The most important thing to remember before you start is to have clarity on the people that may be able to help you. It's fine to ask for advice or help in the business, as long as you are respectful.

Why not write a list of people you know in the dance industry and analyse the list? Is there anyone on that list that may be able to help you? And if so, how? An understanding of how they can help you could be the start of your journey in getting to work closely with the industry.

Once you have the names written down, think about how you will approach them. As opposed to winging it when you meet them, think about what you are going to say to them. This could make all the difference.

When you approach people in the industry, if they sense that you are approaching them because you respect them, they are more likely to help you. However, if they feel like you are asking them as a last resource because you are stuck in the dance industry and you feel like you've run out of ideas, then they are less likely to help you.

No one wakes up before the journey and is successful, they have been where you are and, therefore, in most cases, they will want to help. So, go on and ask for help - why not?

. . . .

Take A Class

Taking class is a good way to get your first set of contacts. Your teacher is likely to know of an event or upcoming auditions that you could be a part of, etc.

I auditioned for a well-known musical and was sure I was one of the strongest. However, I got cut almost immediately. So, I decided to make the most of that day as it had taken me 3 hours to travel to the audition. I went for a class at Pineapple Studios, a choreographer saw me in class and he told me he wanted to see me in an audition. I did the audition and got the part, for quite a big show. Expose yourself as much as you can to working with new teachers and choreographers, as you never know exactly what they are looking for.

I have employed dancers who have come to some of my classes and a few of them I have worked with more than once. Just being in class shows commitment and for potential employers, it showcases dancers that are serious about their profession and are going to work hard for them.

Being in class means you are seen by teachers/ choreographers for an hour and a half, in comparison to the very short time you get to catch the eye of someone on the panel in an audition setting. Choreographers like to use people they know - it feels safer – so, you've got to get your face seen via classes. I know many dancers, including myself, who were hired for many jobs just from taking classes.

"Luck" plays a role in all aspects of life and professions, but those that make their own "Luck" somehow tend to do better. The more I practice, the luckier I am... hmm? If you are attending classes and working towards your goal, then you are aligning yourself with the universe and your vision for landing that job. You will be attracting more opportunities to you as you will be vibrating on a higher energy level and your energy will be where it needs to be in order to be a success.

There are lots of choreographers teaching at places like:
- Pineapple Studio, https://www.pineapple.uk.com
- Danceworks, http://danceworks.net

- Studio 68, http://studio68london.net
- Dance Attic, http://www.danceattic.com
- The Place, http://www.theplace.org.uk
- Big City Dance – Newcastle, https://www.dancecity.co.uk
- Husky Studios, www.huskystudios.co.uk

Trying different classes, with different teachers, is a fantastic way of not only keeping yourself in shape and sustaining your technique, but also to meet new people in the industry.

To make connections that last in classes you have to start by being positive, being aware and giving off the right vibe. This is because your future employer could be in the same room and you want to be seen as someone employable. Make yourself enjoyable to be employable. Who wants to work with a misery guts? Whilst you aren't always going to try to impress everyone, a positive attitude goes a long way.

Being in class also allows you to focus on improving your technique and stamina. If you don't make connections from class, at least gain as much as you can from the lessons because a class is, after all, a place to maintain, improve and stay focused.

It is also a place where you could get help in getting yourself an agent or castings, through information from fellow dancers and teachers. I have helped many good students in the past to get an agent and have also given them information on auditions. I love to help people and there are a lot of others out there who would love to help you too. There are many people at the top of their game that have been in the same position as you are now. They are where they are because they were brave and tried everything they could.

. . . .

Offline and Online Networking

Whilst once in a while dance colleges and university teachers will bring in choreographers, directors, agencies, etc., you cannot always afford to wait for this to happen. You could be proactive and start reaching out to the people you want via other platforms. Going to events to connect with people or using the Internet are two great tools to use.

Why not follow the choreographers' companies you admire or would like to work for in the future? You could like their pages and comment on them as well. It's a great way to connect and it immediately links you to that person or company.

One to watch out for, that wasn't around for me, but deserves a mention is www.thenetworkreveals.com. All you need to know is in their website.

For more information contact@thenetworkrevals.com.

A lot of corporate companies have Events or PR firms that handle events for them. And some of these events require dancers. By visiting http://www.event.org.uk you can find a few companies to reach out to based on the content in their respective website galleries. And by visiting https://www.accessplace.com you can find a directory of PR firms in the UK listed by areas in which they do business.

You can also add yourself to newsletter databases of events via their websites. A few that come to mind include, but aren't limited to:

- Move It Dance - http://www.moveitdance.co.uk
- Breaking Convention - http://www.breakinconvention.com
- Dance Umbrella - http://danceumbrella.co.uk
- Resolution - http://www.theplace.org.uk
- Cloud Dance Festival - http://www.cloud-dance-festival.org.uk
- Edinburgh International Festival - https://www.eif.co.uk
- London Dance - http://londondance.com
- Big Dance - http://www.bigdance.org.uk

Events mean you will be rubbing shoulders with people in the industry and that's likely to motivate you.

Using websites such as https://www.onedanceuk.org, you can find a list of different agencies to reach out to. Go to http://www.thecdg.co.uk where you can also access the hundreds of casting directors out there. Write to them and send them your CV and link to your portfolio or website. Yes, these professionals receive a lot of emails and might never get a chance to read yours. There are steps you can take to stand a better chance of your email being read by them.

Ensure that your e-mail's subject line is compelling. Think of something highly creative, personable and yet professional. Follow up with another 4 – 7 sentences of who you are, a link to your profile and what you would like them to do for you. (Before you send an email to an agent, do research on some of their work, the people they represent, etc.).

Here is an example:

To Whom It May Concern,

My name is Taira Foo. I am a dancer, currently seeking representation. I have attached my CV and, below, you can find links to my work.

Please also have a look at my website www.tairafoo.com.

Let me know if you would like any further information.

Many Thanks,

Taira Foo
Dancer
07XXX XXX XXX
www.tairafoo.com

Links to work:

http://vimeo.com/71110882 - Choreographers showreel

http://vimeo.com/71962095 -The Soloist trailer

http://vimeo.com/71961512 - Rainman trailer

If you are still struggling with getting responses from agencies and directors, don't give up. Keep at it. Just don't harass or stalk them. If you know someone that knows them, then nudge them a little to put in a good word for you. Sometimes it's not what you know, but who you know that might get them to look at your CV. Sometimes it could be that all your emails are going straight into the junk or spam folders because of your email address. There's no point in using an email address like sexydancer@gmail.com instead of using your own name and surname. An email address like "sexy dancer" is likely to be rejected by most servers as containing inappropriate content.

. . . .

FINDING AGENTS

Making connections comes in many formats, as different rules apply to the different genres in the industry. In some cases, you will have to invest a bit of money to get access to information and perhaps a wider network of contacts.

CONTACTS
The essential book of contacts for the entertainment industry.

By purchasing this book you are saving yourself a lot of time that would have gone into online searches. It has information on agencies, casting directors, photographers, training, dance organisations, theatre producers, health and well-being, and promotional services. It's a wealth of information. You can buy the book on www.contactshandbook.com.

SPOTLIGHT

Once you have secured an agent, they will ask you to join Spotlight, if you haven't already.

Casting directors for film, television, theatre, commercials, etc. post castings on Spotlight and either talent agencies can put actors forward or actors can apply directly for consideration. This website allows casting directors, directors and choreographers to access your information.

It will cost you around £150.00 to join the platform. You can read more on it here: https://www.spotlight.com.

MUSICAL THEATRE

I have attended numerous open auditions for musical theatre where I have been successful.

So, if you haven't got an agent at the moment you can still succeed. The advantage of having an agent in this scenario is that you will be in a group of, say, 20 to 30 people rather than it feeling like a cattle market. I have worked with a couple of people who have been very successful and not had an agent, but there aren't many.

There are a few agents to consider and they include, but are not limited to:

- Access
  www.access-uk.com
- Debbie Rimmer
  www.debbierimmer.com
- Michelle Blair
  www.michelleblairmanagement.co.uk
- The Production Exchange
  www.theproductionexchange.com
- Narrow Road Agency
  www.narrowroad.co.uk

CONTEMPORARY FIELD

Whilst most dance fields make use of agents to secure dancers, the contemporary world is quite different.

Going to a company class is great for being seen.

To get to the company classes, you have to send them your CV and request to do a class with them. The companies do receive a lot of these requests, so you will have to be patient and persistent.

You could also do research on touring companies. They don't always go to the popular areas like London, for example. This is also good because you might stand a better chance of securing a place in one of their classes in areas where there aren't many dancers.

The few contemporary dance companies that do use agents

usually use their main source of employing dancers through sites such as:

- Article 19
  http://www.article19.co.uk
- Juice
  http://www.theplace.org.uk/juice
- London Contemporary Dance
  http://www.lcds.ac.uk/lcds-homepage
- Arts Jobs
  http://www.artsjobs.org.uk/dance/
- Mandy Network
  http://www.mandy.com
- Auditions
  www.auditions.com
- Dancing Opportunities
  www.dancingopportunities.com

COMMERCIAL AGENTS

In regards to the commercial world, you still need to get seen, as well as securing an agent.

Why not take a class at Studio 68 (www.studio68london.net), as a lot of commercial choreographers teach there. It's a great place to meet other commercial dancers and hear of upcoming castings or auditions. Keep yourself in the loop and make sure you are always connected with your industry, as it is also easy to let it slip away.

The commercial world is very competitive and is one that needs you to be constantly on point. Make sure you have a strong image in this world - one that will be remembered. In castings, you need to have good photos - men need to look like men and women like women.

There are a few agents to consider and they include:

- Kutes (Jerry Reeves Agency)
  www.jerryreeve.co.uk
- AMCK
  www.amck.tv
- Dancers Inc
  www.dancersincworld.com
- Mass Movement
  www.massmovement.uk.com
- AJK
  www.ajkagency.com
- Headnod
  www.headnodagency.com
- Accelerate
  www.accelerate-productions.co.uk
- Event Model Management
  www.eventmodel.co.uk
- Rudeye Agency
  www.loverudeye.com

• • • • • • • • • • • • • •

Moving Forward with Your Agent(s)

Finding the right agent can help you infinitely to reach your goals. An agent has the experience to help you – they understand how contracts are put together, how to promote you and help you succeed.

Many agents hold auditions now, so if you didn't manage to catch the eye of an agent in your graduation show, like me, then look out for auditions and get one using any means aforementioned.

https://www.facebook.com/groups/HustleCommunity/ often has auditions for agents. Once again, do your research. Just because agencies are auditioning doesn't mean they are going to get you thousands of jobs. Be vigilant and ask around if you're not sure.

Depending on the type of performing artist you are, you can have either one or multiple agents. Dance agencies tend to allow you to have multiple agents. However, if you are with a sole management agency, you can only be on their books. You will probably know what works best for you.

The average that most agents will take from the earnings of each job they get you should be around 12.5%-15% (as of 2017). Never pay anything upfront and, again, always research each agent you choose.

When you do meet with your agent, be honest about the sort of work you want to do. Remember, they work for you, not the other way around. And, if you do not feel comfortable with them, find another agent that you can talk to with ease and have the reassurance that they will be working for you, not doing you a favour.

Should you find yourself with no auditions after signing up with your agent, you need to ask them why. It could be down to your photographs, which you could then change. You have to be learning constantly about what will take you to the next level and then apply it. If you feel like your brand is being taken in a different direction, let your agent know.

Because I have Chinese heritage, my agent put me up for a lot of auditions that were looking specifically for Chinese dancers. However, if you look at my headshot, I don't look Chinese at all. I went to numerous auditions where I felt extremely out of place. I felt I had crashed the audition and the reception from some of the producers was a bit frosty, too. It was not only a waste of their time, but a waste of mine as well. I felt the agent didn't represent me as an artist; it was almost like he was just trying to get me in wherever, regardless of my skills set. I just kept turning up, as I trusted that they had my best interests at heart. I was too afraid to tell him that the parts weren't suitable, as I didn't want to lose representation.

You are valuable! You are unique! You are very different from anyone else in this world. You must value yourself as an artist and then others will do the same. This was a huge learning curve for me, one that I want to pass on to you, so you don't make the same mistake.

You might be feeling that you should say yes to any agent that comes along and offers you representation, but I disagree. Yes, there are a lot of people in our industry and yes it is competitive, but you've come this far, so you may as well make sure you make the right choices when it comes to choosing an agent.

Try to choose an agent that has fewer people on their books, as that will mean more opportunities for you. Make sure there are no long-term contracts between you and the agent and that you can get out of the agreement in a reasonable time to recover if you fall out and they put you on the bottom of the pile.

. . . .

Stay In Touch With Your Agent

If your agent isn't getting you those auditions, you need to be proactive in calling them. I remember one day I was lying on my bed feeling stuck and a bit lost. I hadn't had any auditions for a while and I was still in Derby. I decided to pick up the phone to my agent and asked if there was anything going that I would be suitable for. They replied, "well, we have this new show that's auditioning; they are looking for ..." They could not have described my skill set any better. It had ME written all over it!!! However, they didn't think of me until I called THEM, so they wouldn't have phoned me.

They managed to get me an audition for this show and guess what? It became my first West End show. You don't need to ring your agent everyday, but you just need to take action when you feel it's needed. Can you imagine if I hadn't made that call?

I spent many hours turning up to auditions that weren't appropriate for me - so much so, that I felt embarrassed. Save yourself from that and make sure you are seen for the right roles.

However, if you don't have an agent, DON'T HOLD BACK. Get out there and make a name for yourself. An agent will find you if you are creating enough movement!

"Where there is no heart there is no art," Anna Pavlova.

REMEMBER!

- Connections will take you further than contacts. You have to put in the work to build and maintain these relationships.
- You are the master of your destiny; use every resource available to you and online searches to find the agent, auditions and gigs you want.
- Feel the fear and act on every plan you put to paper. Break everything down so you don't feel overwhelmed and you will do well.
- Don't always go with the first agent. Do your research.

KNOWLEDGE IS POWER!**

Keep learning and empowering yourself through platforms such as:

- http://www.waitingforthecall.co.uk
- https://www.onedanceuk.org
- http://www.thecdg.co.uk
- http://www.event.org.uk
- https://www.accessplace.com

And if you can find the time, it wouldn't hurt to read the following books:

- *How to Win Friends and Influence People* by Dale Carnegie.

You can also get an audio version. It's a great use of time to listen to this when driving or you're in the bath!

**Website links last checked in January 2017.

Photographer: Rolfe Klement

Chapter 5

Auditions

The Basics

You can't control the outcome of your audition, but you can control your experience of it.

The first rule of auditions: never ever miss your audition!

This may sound like common sense and it is, but you'll be surprised how many people slip up - don't be that person. I have been to numerous auditions where the client/ dancer didn't show up. This not only annoys the creative team and audition panel, but also is unfair to other dancers that could have attended the audition.

When a dancer doesn't show up, the panel has one less person to choose from. This is a huge disregard to the amount of time and effort that go into choosing the most appropriate people for the audition. Casting directors, directors, and choreographers spend a lot of time looking through high volumes of photographs and CVs, so when you don't show up, it's a sign of disrespect. Your name will be remembered negatively and could ruin your chances of being seen for something else, which goes back to the effects of your actions on your personal reputation. Always remember that the industry is not as large as you imagine it to be - it's very small and word travels very fast.

When auditioning, always arrive early, behave professionally and stay humble. These are actions that make it easy for people to talk to you, both before and after the audition, and will widen your contacts network. Choreographers and directors want to be able to work with people who are not going to be difficult, so make sure you are aware of your actions; as obvious as it may seem, some people just don't know how they come across.

If you don't have an agent yet, you can find auditions at places like:

- Mandy Network - www.mandy.com

- London Dance - www.londondance.com

- Juice (The Place) - www.theplace.org.uk/juice

- Article 19 - www.article19.org

- The Stage - www.thestage.co.uk

- Pineapple notice board - www.pineapple.uk.com

- Dance Attic notice board - www.danceattic.com

- Pearson Casting Facebook - https://www.facebook.com/pearsoncasting/

- The Hustle Facebook - https://www.facebook.com/groups/HustleCommunity/

- Danceworks notice board - www.danceworks.net

- Husky Studios - http://www.huskystudios.co.uk/

Before attending auditions make sure you research the show/ project and whom you are auditioning for! This also may sound like an obvious thing to do, but so many artists don't do this. Look at the work of the choreographer and director. It will help give you a better idea of what will be expected. It will also help you to feel more confident and you are also learning something new. WIN!!!

Always remember to say thank you after an audition. I am always very grateful for the people who say thank you to me. Don't go out of your way to hang around - once the audition has finished, say thank you and leave the room. The panel will probably want to discuss the audition, who they want, etc. and if you are in the room you are taking up their time.

You could also register on the following sites, especially for contemporary dance:

- www.auditions.com
- www.danceopportunities.com
- www.starnow.com

• • • • • • • • • • • • •

You Can't Fail!

Although getting the job at the end of the audition process is our goal, there are many things we can take away from an audition which will enable us to develop as artists and become more knowledgeable, both mentally and physically.

If you look at an audition as a way of learning it will help you look at the positives. During a recent audition, I took away a wealth of information, something I could pass on to my students. There were things that were said by the choreographer that I hadn't thought about before, so how can this be a negative experience? Another WIN!!!

Look at what you can gain. A lot of my inspiration when embarking on my dance career came from other dancers. If I liked something about a way a dancer moved, I embodied it into my own movement. Rather than being envious of a way a dancer moved, I was inspired. This will also make your journey a happier one. The biggest mistake so many dancers make is comparing themselves to others. If we are constantly comparing ourselves to others then we will be constantly disappointed and our belief in ourselves will rapidly diminish.

Before I sang for auditions, I managed to get myself in a zone where I wasn't listening to the other people that sang before me. I knew I was never the best singer, but I knew I was good enough for the job. I had other skills and so do you! You never really know what they are looking for, so go into the room not only with a positive mindset to learn from the experience, but also knowing that you are good enough. Self-belief plays the biggest part in this journey.

An ex-student, Joshua Ivey, came into dance late, at the age of 16. I remember the very first day he came into the studios - he was very raw, but had the belief & determination from day one. "In my career I found that motivation is one of the hardest things to maintain; the ups and downs of the industry can take you on a constant rollercoaster of highs, middles and lows, leaving you feeling exhausted physically, mentally and emotionally - and that is why it is very vital to understand the importance of self-motivation and using both positive and negative things around you, constructively, to build you into a stronger and smarter performer. To any aspiring performers, my advice to you is to keep going, always work to push outside anything familiar or comfortable, always re-adjust your mindset, positively, to your circumstances, maintain your originality and don't give up. Nothing comes easy, but the rewards are priceless."

Josh worked extremely hard, everyday, and was known to have his dynaband out regularly on the bus, to work on his flexibility. Josh's credits include: *Thriller Live* (West End), *American Assassin* (Feature Film), World of Dance UK Winner's Circle 2015, as well as commercials including Jaguar, House Of Fraser & the O2 (just to name a few).

Debbie O'Brien, a London-based Casting Director, says of auditions, "When we are choosing people for auditions, we look to see where they have trained, and whether they have the right skills for the job – so, they need to have experience or training in the appropriate styles of dance and often they need to sing well. If they don't have the right information on their CV, we probably won't bring them in. Some people are a better fit for some productions than others. They need to have really good headshots, and if they have links to showreels or clips from their previous work, it's always useful,"

• • • • • • • • • • • • •

Feedback From Auditions

You should always get a "thank you" at the end of the day, but after the audition, if you are not successful, you probably won't hear anything.

I have attended many auditions in my career. I have been cut in the first round, got right down to the finals, have had 7-hour auditions, and others were over a few days. As artists, we expect to have zero contact after the audition, not even a "Thank you, we have now cast this role". We spend days, even weeks, preparing songs, scripts, and we may even invest in a couple of singing/ acting lessons to help us.

I remember after that 7-hour day, I sat by the phone for a week waiting for the phone to ring and each day I got closer to the realisation that I probably wasn't going to get the job. I felt exhausted and my vision of being in that particular show started to fade. "How could they keep me there for 7 hours and not even contact me after?" I learned hard and fast that this is just what happens. This is something we have to deal with without taking it personally. It would be great to have closure, so we can move on, but we must simply take a deep breath and look for the next opportunity.

. . . .

The High and Lows

Auditions can stir up many emotions, as there is an incredible energy around them. They are EXCITING and when you are in the midst of it all, it can be almost EUPHORIC! When you are in the zone, music bursting out of the speakers, your adrenaline pumping, you are likely to feel unstoppable!

At the end of the audition, when you are nervously waiting for your name to be called out, holding your breath every time a name that begins with the same letters as yours is spoken, and they reach the end of the list, but your name still hasn't been called, you feel like *"well, they must have made a mistake! Maybe, they didn't see me! Am I in the wrong group? Do they even know I am here? I must have been hidden behind the girl in the green tights".* Your energy levels plummet - what goes up must come down, so you find yourself in a whirl of despair wondering how this could have been?

Internally we have to deal with this. How do we make it easier on ourselves? How can we deal with rejection? I found the more auditions I did, the less painful it got. However, there is always an element of emotions that you just can't help because we are all human. We can, however, use certain methods and tools to make it less painful. I will talk more about this in my next book *The Dancer's Mind*.

The IMPORTANT thing is to not take it personally - it's not you, it's them! You are just not right at this moment in time, so go out there and find someone whose project is the perfect fit for you - maybe someone that's not looking for the girl in the green tights, because there will be many people you will be right for and a lot of people you are just not going to be. A lot of it depends on timing.

Try this exercise after your audition, if you are feeling overwhelmed:

Breathe in and out and concentrate only on your breathing. If you do this it's impossible for you to think about anything else.

The more you do it, the faster you can calm down after auditions and disappointing results.

What To Wear For Auditions

Musical Theatre Auditions

Look at the style of the show - is it jazz, contemporary or hip-hop? Based on that, take things into account and wear something that reflects the style of the show, something that compliments you and shows you off best.

For both boys and girls, wear something colourful and shows you to your best - something that suits your body. If you are going for shows like Chicago or Cats, people tend to wear something tight and black, as they show your figure off.

Girls need to go a step beyond by having manageable hair, but that can still be styled.

Remember to do your research on the show to make sure you know what's appropriate, as well as looking at the breakdown to see what is expected. Always stay one step ahead!

Contemporary Auditions

For either gender, your clothes have to embrace movement.

For boys, wear something colourful. Often, tight tops and looser bottoms work the best.

For girls, contemporary dancers dress very differently. Whilst clothes can still embrace your movement, little make-up usually does the magic. Wearing a lot of make-up when going to a contemporary company audition could make you look out of place. Still, wear make-up, but stay away from the lashes.

Commercial Auditions

Fashionable and tight clothes, very styled and with make-up on is great. Just make sure you know you can dance in your outfit because we've all witnessed that someone who has "fallen out" of their top.

The same applies to boys. Look fashionable and very styled in your tight clothes. Make sure you are still you - don't become someone else. You are enough as you are.

Think high fashion clothes that show your body beautifully and have your face and hair almost camera–ready.

Ballet Auditions

Classical attire consisting of leotards and tights is the norm. You could wear something baggy over the top, as you can never really know for sure what each company is looking for. What might suit one company might not suit another. Above all, feel comfortable and wear something that makes you feel good.

All in all, always bring everything with you to an audition. Bring every type of shoe because you never know what they might throw at you, even when the brief doesn't say so. Remember to live by Edith Head's words, "you can have anything you want in life if you dress for it."

● ●

"The more auditions you go on, the more you will learn not to take it personally," Paula Abdul.

REMEMBER!

- Never miss an audition.
- Believe in yourself despite the audition outcome.
- Embrace the NOs - they are preparing you for the future YESs.
- Dress for the part you would like to get. Dress for success.

KNOWLEDGE IS POWER!**

Keep learning and empowering yourself through platforms such as:

- http://www.danceforall.co.uk

And if you can find the time, it wouldn't hurt to read the following book:

- *A Ballerina For Our Time: Olga Pavlova* by Karen McDonough.

**Website links last checked in January 2017.

Photographer: Rolfe Klement

Chapter 6

Living a Balanced Life

In this business, we have a lot of juggling to do. Performers often have to balance work and auditions. We can be running from one audition to the next, performing at current gigs, training, rehearsing, eating healthily, working part-time, and trying to stay on top of our budget. Life can be challenging.

So how do we do juggle it all? We need to prioritise what is important to us.

You have to make peace with the fact that your time is precious and there will be times when you will need to be selfish in order to stay in shape, physically, intellectually, emotionally and spiritually for your career. You will need it to eat healthily, enjoy more hours of sleep and nourish your soul and mind without losing human connection.

· · · · · · · · · · · · · ·

Your Health

Dancers are like athletes - we need to be in good health. Dance is constantly evolving and choreography is becoming more athletic by the minute, so we need to make sure we can meet today's high physical demands.

Due to the repetitive strain on muscles and joints, dancers suffer from injuries as much as, say, football players do. Yes, it's that easy and frequent, especially as you grow older.

Whilst there are a lot of things that you could do as a dancer to avoid recurring injuries, such as a balanced diet, adequate rehydration, proper warm-up and cool-down, and deep tissue sports massages, most injuries can be avoided by simply knowing your body well.

Should you get injured and you are on a job, there are moments when you can push through and there are moments when masking the pain might not be the best decision for your career. Speak up! Communicate! Let your director or choreographer know that you are in pain and seek medical help. When you do speak up, it is important to remember that the objective of speaking out is to allow your body to heal and also to be back at work ASAP. That requires a positive mindset, composure, and a controlled tone. Due to time pressures, there may be choreographers that feel anxious about you being injured – take that with a pinch of salt and stay positive. Injuries happen all the time in this business and you are not the first to experience it.

• • • • • • • • • • • • •

Treating Dance Injuries

Whilst some dancers are lucky enough to never experience injuries, most of us will at some point during our careers. Long-performance hours, after strenuous hours of rehearsals, do eventually take their toll on the body. Add to that risk factors such as the surfaces you practice and perform on, such as cold rooms and hard floors, and your joints and muscles are bound to soak up all the stress.

There are, however, ways to manage all this pressure on your body and reduce the long-term effects of the injuries. Some of them include:

- Taking turmeric for inflammation.
- Bathing in magnesium salts after rehearsals.
- Deep tissue or sports massages once or twice a month.
- Making use of foam rollers to relax your muscles.

Beyond the above rehabilitative tips, there are obvious things that we should be doing daily, like warming up before rehearsals and/ or performances; cooling down; staying hydrated; eating well, and sleeping enough hours.

Should you get injured during training, rehearsal or performance, the National Institute of Dance Medicine and Science (NIDMS) has 3 NHS dance clinics in London, Birmingham, and Bath.

The NIDMS website provides all the information of the GPs that you can ask your GP to refer you to based on your injuries.

- For more information on how to get a referral, visit the NIDMS website, https://www.nidms.co.uk, call them on +44(0) 20 7713 0730 or email manager@nidms.co.uk.

It may also be beneficial to investigate alternative therapies, which offer holistic approaches to injury prevention and treatment. Research the practitioners and try various therapies to see which works best for you. These may include:

- Acupuncture (https://www.acupuncture.org.uk/)
- Chiropractic (https://chiropractic-uk.co.uk/)
- Physiotherapy (http://www.csp.org.uk/)
- Reflexology (http://www.aor.org.uk/)
- Osteopathy (https://www.osteopathy.org.uk/home/)
- Reiki (https://www.reikiassociation.net/home.php)

· · · · · · · · · · · · ·

Managing Your Time

Because of the fast pace at which we live our lives today, it is very easy to fall into the trap of perpetual multitasking. Whilst there are activities that work well with multitasking, such as reading or checking the news on the bike at the gym, most daily activities to get ahead require a single-minded focus to have a quality product in the end. You are human, not a machine.

Managing your time requires that you always plan ahead.

Just like me, I am sure of many of you have had unproductive days. This has been because I didn't plan. I would have more or less just wandered through my day without actually being productive. The days that have worked in my favour, that have made me feel good and in line with my goals, are when I have planned them. An example would be the time spent on social media, or the Internet in general, consuming other people's lives without really achieving anything. According to The Telegraph UK (May 2015), young adults were spending up to 27 hours per week online in 2014. These are scary statistics, but you could easily become one of them if you are not conscious of what you are spending your time on.

Ending each day by writing what you would like to accomplish, or simply do, the following day, reduces the amount of thinking you have to do upon waking up. In a way, it allows you to start the day on a positive note. Forbes.com has so many articles on how successful people always plan their days ahead of time.

It is important, however, when planning for the following day, to be realistic. There are only 24 hours in a day. So your to-dos should be realistically aligned to that. Failure to do so and you could find yourself with an unfinished list every day, which could lead to frustration. Frustration could push you back into the old habits of never planning for the day ahead and we don't want this.

Try to plan for each day until it becomes a habit. Scientifically, habits don't require you to do any thinking; again, this takes away the sense of being overwhelmed, which is what we want to achieve.

· · · · · · · · · · · · · ·

STAYING FIT

It is very important to keep up your training. You are an athlete and you need to make sure you are maintaining your body to its highest function. It's very easy to lose years of training through long breaks from class.

At college, some of you will have trained for hours and hours a day. After graduation, your schedule changes dramatically, so you need to make sure that all those years are not lost. If you are serious about a dance career, then you will have to make sure you are on top of your game! If you don't, there will be others working very hard, daily, and they will be the ones securing jobs.

Staying fit will also make you feel better, especially on the days when you feel a bit out of touch, as we all have these moments.

Because your body is your career's equipment, you have to treat it with grace and love. Pushing yourself through running, Yoga, Pilates, and weights training at the gym are all great, as long as you can respect what your body tells you. It is one thing to dream of doing an ultra-marathon, but you have to understand the impact of that training on your body. Whilst yoga is good for relaxing your body and mind, not to mention the flexibility, there are different types of yoga, such as Ashtanga, that are pretty good for high-intensity workouts. There is also Bikram, which will help you stretch your muscles and increase flexibility, which, of course, is always a good thing in our industry.

The beauty of the modern life is that if you can't afford a membership to participate in any of the fitness classes that you like, there are Apps everywhere offering them. Please remember that trying a new form of fitness regime on your own could get you injured, so again, know thy body and know when to stop. If you are unsure, seek the help of a specialist.

Deep tissue sports massages once or twice a month will also help your muscles recover easily. And never forget the good old ice bath when you know you've pushed your body a bit too much on any given day.

Magnesium salts are a wonderful way of repairing sore muscles. You can bathe in these and they will reduce the aches and pains. If you are about to go into a big rehearsal schedule, then I recommend you invest in some of these - it will make all the difference. When you exert your body physically, through dance or exercise, you could end up with lactic acid build-up. This is what causes soreness in muscles. Epsom salts help in extracting that acid out of your body, so you wake up refreshed the following day.

· · · · · · · · · · · · · ·

NUTRITION

We are athletes and we need to keep ourselves in the best condition. I know with the fast pace of life, it can sometimes be hard to eat well. Grabbing the nearest and cheapest thing is all too easy to do and can become a slippery slope.

It's easy to think that because you train hard every day and you are not overweight, then you can eat everything you want and have a healthy body. Eating healthily doesn't have to be a daunting exercise; it's an easier lifestyle, once adopted. Because your body takes on so much strain, it needs to recover. Eating well will allow your muscles, bones, and joints to carry you for more years in the industry.

The most budgetary and healthy way to live is by eating clean. By eating clean you will be able to incorporate into your life all the nutrients that your body needs to have more energy levels, focus and concentration when you both practice and perform. In addition, good-looking skin from eating well will likely increase your confidence. Clean eating that covers most of the nutrients that your body needs to function at its highest potential usually consists of foods from these groups: carbohydrates, protein, fats, vitamins and minerals, and water.

I know it's obvious, but water is a must and you should be carrying a bottle with you everywhere you go and refill it when it runs out. By so doing, you save yourself money on buying water and you also won't forget to drink it if it's always on you. Scientifically, most adults require up to 2 litres of water a day. However, because your career means you will sweat a lot, you should be drinking more to stay hydrated, avoid headaches, and help your body digest food better.

Without overwhelming you, below are some foods from each group that you should try to incorporate into your diet:

Carbohydrates
- Buckwheat
- Coconut flour
- Sorghum
- Brown/ wild rice
- Low GI bread
- Sweet potatoes
- Quinoa
- Bulgur wheat
- Couscous
- Pearl barley
- Pumpkin

Protein

- Eggs
- Chicken
- Meat
- Tofu
- Greek yoghurt
- Almonds
- Cottage cheese
- Milk
- Turkey
- Broccoli
- Lentils
- Salmon

Vitamins & Minerals

- Chickpeas
- Swordfish
- Fruits
- Vegetables
- Peanuts
- Trout
- Milk
- Beans
- Sunflower seeds
- Sardines

Fats

- Wild salmon
- Flax seeds
- Olive oil
- Avocado
- Walnuts
- Duck
- Walnuts
- Meat
- Cheese
- Olives

Please note that this isn't a conclusive list, it's just meant to guide you, based on my experiences. There are other foods that fall into the four categories that you can still consume. As long as food is eaten in moderation and it provides the body with necessary nutrients, then you should be fine.

It is, however, ideal to reduce as much artificial sugars as possible from your life. As opposed to a store-bought juice or soft drink, a home-made smoothie or juice would be better. You will get more nutrients and energy, without feeling lethargic after.

And if you aren't sure about what you are eating and its nutritional value, ask your nutritionist or look up what http://www.webmd.com has to say. Because professional medical practitioners put the content together, it is one of the few websites I trust health-wise.

Eating well requires some cooking on your part and with the volumes of recipes on Pinterest, the web, and various Apps, you can put together healthy meals in a short space of time. Here are a few that I would recommend:

Change4Life, Smart Recipes (by the NHS, free on iOS and Android)

Pepper Plate, Recipe, Menu and Cooking Planner (free on iOS and Android)

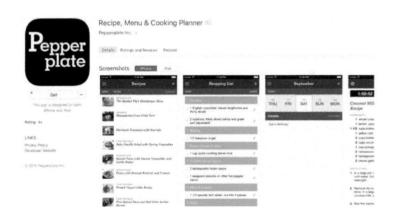

At the end of the day, your diet is like a bank account and, in Bethenny Frankel's words, "just as you balance your spending and savings, you must balance your food choices. Don't eat too much of any one thing, don't eat the same thing twice, balance starches with proteins, vegetables, and fruits with sweets, always balance a splurge with a save."

Whilst you might be shopping, cooking and eating well, let's face it, your lifestyle is pretty different. You don't always get the break at the same time, like an office-bound professional. You will have days of unending free time and days of no breaks. This is where the willpower to stay the journey comes in. Instead of getting caught unprepared and ending up eating crap, put nuts and healthy snacks in your bag. My favourite healthy snack has to be boiled eggs and a banana - they work like magic. Snacks save you a lot from eating unhealthily. Just as much as you commit to carrying water with you everywhere, also try to commit to carrying snacks on you, including when you travel. I cannot even begin to tell you of the number of posts on social media, especially Pinterest, about the snacks you can take on a road trip or a plane to save both your wallet and your body from eating decisions that will haunt you. So go on, do the research and find snacks that work for you and always, always have them at hand.

And if cooking isn't really your thing, there are other ways you can eat well and within a tight budget. I have never considered cooking to be my strength, especially when it's only me I am cooking for. I want to eat something fast and tasty, that's going to give me the energy I need. The list below requires little or no cooking at all. They won't break your bank balance either. They work well for a small budget. You can mix them up, depending on how much activity you do. I normally just increase or decrease the portions. Listen to your body; listen to what it needs in order to perform to your best:

- Tuna
- Boiled eggs
- Nuts
- Super seeds on top of porridge
- Porridge
- Asparagus

- Prawns
- Blueberries
- Spinach
- Tomatoes
- Cottage cheese
- Avocado

• • • • • • • • • • • • • •

Mindfulness

Everything in life that is monumental or life-changing requires a lot of mental strength. So will your career. But what is mental strength? Personally, for me, it's to accept what is and ultimately carry on with a positive mentality, even when it seems unrealistic. It's the grit to keep moving forward, even when it feels futile. Remember Mandela's words, "it all seems impossible until it's done." Well, look at everything that happens through your life and career that way.

Your mind can be both your best and worst ally, at the same time. Just think of any ordinary day in your life - who questions and supports you the most? Yourself. How? Through your mind. You have a choice on whether your mind becomes your best friend or your worst enemy. My next book, *The Dancer's Mind* will look at this further, so, for now, let's stick to what can help you. No one has the power to destroy you, but you. Your thoughts become you.

Because you are a dancer, it doesn't mean that the effects of life's pressures which you face every day are different from what a teacher, homeless person, doctor, president, etc. are any different. It's all relative to each individual's journey. The way to deal with those pressures mentally is the same.

The ability to manage mental pressure builds resilience and will help you to manage stress better. The less stressed you are, the more you will be able to focus on your career and set yourself up for success.

So how do you build mental resilience?

 You have to stop worrying about things that you can't control. Just because you fell yesterday at rehearsal, it isn't guaranteed that you will fall tomorrow during your performance. It's okay to feel nervous, but it doesn't help you if it keeps you awake and you have to face the next day without having rested your body and mind. I always say that we like to write stories in our heads - stories that may never come true. Have you ever tried to listen to your body when you are stressed? Your heart races, you can't focus, you can't taste what you are eating and the ability to laugh at the funniest joke disappears. It's almost as if your body is going into uncontrollable shock. You don't need that. Focus on the positive by **visualising** what you would like tomorrow to be. Imagine what that success is going to feel like and allow that feeling to take over your mind, body, and emotions.

2 Sometimes, no matter how much you visualise what you would like your tomorrow or future to be like, the stress might not go away. I live by **meditation** and it could work for you. It is important to remember that meditation is not a religion and you can practice it without feeling guilty that you are going against your core beliefs. Whilst it might be difficult in the beginning to sit in complete silence, focusing on your breathing and nothing else, you will get there eventually. And, if thoughts keep coming into your head, acknowledge them, release them and go back to focusing on your breathing until you have the art nailed down. Meditation allows you to focus on the present and to live in the now, which will save you energy to perform better. Being able to acknowledge thoughts or feelings and choosing to let them go through meditation equips you to handle rejection, bad days and losses in a more positive way. As a dancer, you are constantly giving pieces of yourself to your audience. Meditation is the nourishment you need to give yourself - to refresh your mind, body, and soul.

Here are guided meditations that can help you; they are available on YouTube:

- Jason Stephenson
- Oprah & Deepak Chopra 21-day meditation Challenge-perfect health
- Guided Breathing meditation with Kim Eng

3 A positive mindset will allow you to handle your daily actions towards reaching your career goals in a less overwhelming way. However, that requires you to be highly **organised and focused**. When you are organised, focused and know what you aim to achieve every single day, as soon as you wake up, you are training your mind to get used to a certain routine that, in the long run, becomes habit. Try it for a few days by starting with, say, three things that you would like to achieve tomorrow. When you've completed them, doesn't it feel great? Go with four things for the day after and continue, until being organised gets you excited over other things, besides dancing, you would like to accomplish. If you don't finish everything on a bad day, that's fine, smile and start again the following day.

4 Practice **gratitude**. When you constantly see the good and privileges you already have, as opposed to focusing on what you don't have or can't do, you will feel much happier with your own life and journey. It is this inner happiness that will anchor you to remain humble as you become successful, but most importantly, you stop taking your mind, body, and soul through the trauma of all the negative words and actions you will come across in life in general. An attitude of gratitude has the power to make you glow from within; in return, you become happier in all areas of your life. It takes 21 days to see the benefits from this, so why not start now?

A great TED Talk, that focuses on gratitude as the key to happiness can be watched on YouTube:

- http://www.ted.com/talks/shawn_achor_the_happy_secret_to_better_work

Lastly, find yourself a **support** system, network or base. Just as you support your family and certain friends in different ways, you need to build your own support system. You will face physical, intellectual, emotional, and spiritual challenges throughout your career. You need to be aware of who you can trust with, say, financial problems. When your performance is found lacking, who can give you a pep talk and help cheer you on? Not every friend, family member or industry connection will serve the same purpose in your career and you need to understand that.

• • • • • • • • • • • • •

LIVE

Whilst performing is the career you've chosen and you will be living and breathing it most of the time, it is imperative to have a life outside the dance industry. If I could go back and give myself one piece of advice, it would be to not forget to enjoy the journey. It's an incredible one, but it pays to be aware that there's more to life. You know that quote, *"no one is busy all the time, it's just what you prioritise"*? Make time for your friends and family, as they will help keep you sane during the hard times and are also a reminder of how beautiful life is.

sTime away from dance, physically and mentally, helps you appreciate it more when you do get back to it. It will also give you space in your head. There was a time when all I focused on was dance. It almost became an addiction and I couldn't be happy without it. I know now how more enjoyable life could have been had I enjoyed it with people around me, those that embraced my journey rather than be hard on myself.

I can't regret it now, as it has enabled me to become the person I am today, but I would like you to enjoy the journey. Take time to visit places and laugh with those that you love. We are extremely blessed to do what we love, but need to stay balanced in order to perform at our best.

Balance also works in different ways. When you start working on a show you will find that you have a lot of time off during the day. This is time to connect, genuinely, with others in the industry. Often after performing you wind down the adrenaline and excitement with a drink. The drink could, however, take away that time you have in the day to relax with others, if you don't end it at one or two. Getting home early hours of the morning, sleeping in until late afternoon and missing important things like rehearsals, etc. could, in the end, become a self-destructive vicious cycle that's hard to break. Everything in moderation – balance is simply that.

"Believe in yourself and all that you are. Know that there is something inside you that is greater than any obstacle," Christian Larson.

REMEMBER!

- Eat well and be kind to your body. You will never regret it.
- Keep up your fitness levels and techniques.
- Enough sleep is good for you.
- Have a positive mindset, despite what life brings your way.

KNOWLEDGE IS POWER!**

Keep learning and empowering yourself through platforms such as:

- http://thedailypositive.com
- http://www.positivelypositive.com
- https://www.youtube.com/user/ILoveJuicyShow (guided meditation by Jason Stephenson)
- The Movie/Documentary – DANCER featuring Sergei Polunin 2016 – Directed by Steven Cantor

And if you can find the time, it wouldn't hurt to read the following books:

- *The Power Of Now* by Eckhart Tolle
- *What is Meditation* by Eckhart Tolle

**Website links last checked in January 2017.

Photographer: Garry Lake

Chapter 7

Rejection Redefined

This is probably one of the hardest things to deal with. Unfortunately, it happens to all of us at some point. It's even more difficult when you have a number placed on you, only to be cut in the first round. You feel you didn't really have a fair chance, no one from the panel looked at you, and you strongly believe if they had, they would have seen something.

The cold hard fact that you will have to accept again and again is that you will never really know what the audition panels are looking for. I have been to many auditions and thought they were some of my strongest, yet I was often cut straight away. I didn't understand why - why they didn't see me, see my attack and energy, and PASSION? I mean come on? Listen, don't take it personally!

Rejection could be just a matter of you being too small or too tall to fit the role they need a dancer for. I have sat on an audition panel with a producer saying to me, "she won't fit in the hat... she won't fit in the boots". I mean, for crying out loud, can't you just get another costume? It was sitting on that audition panel that made me realise just how bizarre this world, the performing arts industry, is – so, just don't take it personally and don't give up!

The next time you get cut, smile and remember that that NO is taking you closer to your YES! I know it's not related to dance, but think of Thomas Edison - he made more than 10,000 attempts before he finally managed to refine the light bulb. If he had given up, would we have lights today? Maybe, but someone would have had to pick up where he left off and try again and again. Michael Jordan missed over 9,000 shots at goal. Every rejection, you need to view as a stepping-stone and a lesson for your next job.

The best way for me to deal with rejection is to go and do something that has a positive impact. We all feel better after a great class don't we? I have taken classes that have literally made me feel like I was flying afterward, so rather than making yourself feel worse about a situation by constantly trying to analyse what went wrong, be kind to yourself and do something that will make you feel better.

Find an outlet that works for you. Use it and centre yourself again for the next opportunity. Try to take as much positivity from the audition as you can.

. . . .

Redefining Rejection

Whilst rejection is rejection, the word itself doesn't sit right with me. I think we need to change it. When your skill set and image is not right for a particular project or show, then we must simply move on to the next opportunity and use this as an experience we can learn from, rather than saying we were rejected.

So many dancers lose their confidence and motivation through a constant thread of NOs. This can be hard to deal with, but we must accept it as part of our industry. There is no other industry like it.

I understand how it feels when you constantly have to go back to your family and friends and tell them it was another NO. I understand that those close to you may be thinking "well, he/ she will have to think about doing something else soon". Or, you might be thinking that the rejections, in their minds, mean that you aren't good enough, if you keep getting rejected. This is probably how the majority of us feel, so know that you are not alone and that these feelings are very normal.

I think this was the hardest part for me. My endless journeys from Derby to London for numerous auditions; my family took me to the station at 5am and they were waiting for me when I got back. It was even harder when I had to go through the whole scenario with them and try to get them to understand that this is what happens. Fortunately, they were always very supportive. I used to feel like I had let them down. I could feel a churning in my stomach knowing that I would have to go back and tell them it was another NO.

As artists, we put so much pressure on ourselves. I remember when I used to get an audition and thought, 'well this is it; this is the one!' I had great feelings about it, imagined myself in the role, imagined people coming to see me, and even imagined going back to my parents telling them I had got the job. So, automatically, I had put all of this pressure onto myself and I know that you will also be doing this, too. Why do we do it? We absolutely don't need to. It's a habit I had developed, but one that needed to disappear.

In a recent audition, I decided to apply some of my self-development training to dealing with the scenario. I started to focus on each moment at a time. I took every moment and became present in it. By this, I mean I wasn't thinking about how this job could change my life, make me a better person, a more employable person, how many people could come and see me, or what that phone call to my loved ones was going to feel like once I had the job. I was just thinking about that moment. As I put my trainers on for the audition I concentrated and focused on each lace, felt my feet in the soles and began to warm up. This really helped me focus. And I think this will help you, too. Don't think about what the job could give you; don't think about how it will change your life; just accept it for what it is. It is an audition and a chance for you to demonstrate to the panel whether you can help them or not in telling their story to an audience.

While writing this book I realised I had been out of touch as an auditionee for a while.

Last week I decided to audition for a musical. I hadn't auditioned for many years and the thought absolutely petrified me, but I knew in order for me to help you I needed to do this. Since committing to the audition I began to think about the "what ifs" and started putting huge pressure on myself. I was creating, in my mind, things that hadn't happened yet and my emotions were like a series of fireworks. Every time I did this and became aware of my emotions, I brought myself into the present moment and constantly doing this helped me focus. In my next book, *The Dancers Mind*, I will talk more about this.

You can always handle what is given to you at that moment, but it would be very difficult to handle what you think will happen.

There are a few things that I found to be very helpful to be able to stay positive. These include:

- Music – put a good piece of music on.
- Singing – singing sends energy vibrations around your body that will make you feel good.
- Class or exercise – the endorphins released trigger a positive feeling in the body.
- Friends – hang out with a friend and share a laugh.

In essence, do something enjoyable, rather than cutting yourself off from the world. This will only lower your good vibrations.

• • • • • • • • • • • • • •

WHAT OTHERS THINK

It's very easy for me to say 'don't worry about what others think' because, for some reason, we all do - especially in this industry where our bodies and minds are our instruments. We are our business, so we can take things very personally when we haven't been cast or are cut immediately in an audition.

Many people are driven by what others think. I have been one of these people and, if I am honest, I can still catch myself doing things because of what others think.

I used to worry about what my peers would think. I felt on a high when things went well and couldn't wait to tell everyone, but when things didn't work out I could barely make eye contact with anyone. Even though it wasn't as strong as the word I am using, there was an element of shame. Why? Why are we embarrassed? We weren't right for the job. Why can't I make eye contact with someone just because I hadn't been right for something?

You must try not to feel like this - it will suck your energy and demotivate you and right now we need all the motivation we can get.

It doesn't matter to anyone else. You just need to focus on how this experience can help develop you, whether that is through gaining strength to become stronger mentally or simply being in a room that has a wonderful energy and excitement about it. Stand tall for the fact you have chosen to do something you love. This, on its own, is completely admirable!

You see if we turn things around in our minds and look for the positives in the experience, then we can start to change the way we think about things

Life is short, so you must not spend it beating yourself up. Look for things you can enjoy out of it. This is a wonderful business - take the things you thought were negative and turn them into positives.

It is not only about your journey as a dancer, it is also your journey as a person. Yes, it's important to focus and be passionate about what you do, but don't forget to look up now and then and be grateful for everything you have, which includes family, friends, and the fact you were brave enough to work for something that is so important to you.

• • • • • • • • • • • •

Why Rejection Might Be Good For You

There was a show I auditioned for in which I got down to the finals. After about three rounds of auditions, it was down to just two of us. It was West End and, boy, was I perfect for this role! I could almost see my name in the programme. I really wanted this show; I mean I really, really wanted it! After the audition, they said thank you and we both waited patiently for the phone to ring. I stared at the phone for two days and each hour that passed by made my heart sink more and more. I finally received a phone call to say maybe next time. MAYBE NEXT TIME? WTF! I was distraught, angry and sad. I was everything apart from being in a secure job. It was the end of the world and every ounce of motivation had escaped rapidly from my body.

The girl who got the job over me was interviewed in a famous dance magazine about her landing the part in the show. Apparently, she couldn't believe she got it either. OMG this was just too much to take!

And, of course, the anticipation from family and friends, to then only watch their faces drop quickly. Although they were smiling, I could see their sympathetic pain. How could this happen, again? Was I ever going to get anywhere? Was anything going to happen?

YES!! It wasn't long until I landed myself a wonderful job, which was a wonderful experience. It didn't last for long and this then took me to my first West End show with an ORIGINAL CAST! This wouldn't have happened if I had secured the other job. So, just keep going; don't give up - the universe has plans for you, I promise! Sometimes rejection is good for you - it opens up space for jobs that you will enjoy more.

There isn't an artist alive that got every gig the first and every time. JK Rowling went to 12 publishers with her book about a wizard and all 12 rejected her. Today, she has enough money to buy all of those publishers out and has entertained millions of people. She is also the first person to drop out of the Forbes Top 100 Richest People because she has given so much of her wealth away. So, who was the better person - JK Rowling or the person at the publishing house, whom, by the way, is probably still there today, commuting in the rush hour, ready to reject some more books? Give it some thought.

When attending an audition, look at the numbers. Let's say there are 100 going for the job and they want 10. The vast majority, 90%, will be rejected! That cannot mean 90% are not good enough. If it did, there would be no dance industry at all. It means that the 10% that made the cut stood out on that day and performed exactly as the panel wanted. The girl in the bright green tights got lucky that day! You'll be back...

"Let go of ego and live fearlessly," Taira Foo.

REMEMBER!

- Being rejected isn't always a reflection of who you are.
- Don't quit your journey because of a NO! Keep going.
- Live in the now and find the positives out of what life throws your way.

KNOWLEDGE IS POWER!**

Keep learning and empowering yourself through platforms such as:

- http://www.motivationalwellbeing.com

And if you can find the time, it wouldn't hurt to read the following book:

- The Power of Positive Living by Norman Vincent Peale.
- Big Magic: Creative Living Beyond Fear by Elizabeth Gilbert

**Website links last checked in January 2017.

Chapter 8

Be Nice

As you build your career, there are going to be highs and lows. This is the same with any other industry, however, because we are so in tune with our emotions and we are constantly having to draw on them in order to perform our work, they can easily rise when put through gruelling rehearsal schedules and challenging choreography. It's really important that we learn to manage our emotions. There will be times when you are so tired you can barely speak, you will wake up in the morning feeling like you have been hit by a bus, your body hurts and aches as you are getting used to a new style of choreography. Through it all, the way you engage with others needs to contribute POSITIVELY to YOU.

Like every industry, there are challenges that you will face. Issues such as choreography that could put extra strain on your body, rejection, ego, fitness, financial demands, peer pressure, people that are difficult to work with, or staying level-headed when successful will all require some sort of interaction between you and others. Do you know what to do in each situation? Whilst I might not have all the answers, there are a few areas where my experience might be of help to you.

• • • • • • • • • • • • •

Stay Humble

You are securing the jobs, you are performing well, others see your success, everything is falling into place and you don't foresee anything going wrong in the near future. You are becoming more confident, and that's great! There is, however, a very fine line between confidence and arrogance. Arrogance will drive your ego! Your ego could turn you into the difficult person that no one wants to work with.

I have seen many extremely talented dancers and worked with some of them. They worked incredibly hard and were wonderful to work with. However, there has also been the odd occasion when I worked with people and chose not to work with them ever again, as I felt uncomfortable with some of their behaviour.

I have been on panels, where I have really liked a performer and the panel knows someone who knew them and said, "I heard they are a nightmare to work with," so we swiftly move on. It doesn't matter how talented someone is, if you are going on tour or working with someone for six months, you don't want to be spending that much time with people who are going to make that experience a horrible one.

· · · · · · · · · · · · ·

It's a Small World

Everyone says it and it's so true! Everyone does know everyone; this industry is like no other. This is why it is so important to stay humble, be kind and work hard. There will always be someone who knows you. Trust me on that one.

Once you have a job with a good company, remember to work well with choreographers and directors. They are likely to be getting other work and if they like you and the way you work, they may keep you in mind for future jobs, as they would rather work with someone they know. Also, it saves them time re-auditioning and having to start from scratch. They want to work with someone that's easy to work with, rather than those they have to take a risk on.

I have always been asked back or asked to do another contract by every one of the companies I have worked with. This was not by accident. I worked hard, stayed humble and I was good to the people around me.

Learn to celebrate your peers' successes as if they were your own - it will make your life a lot more enjoyable! These are attributes that we all want in a cast/ company member.

I worked on a cruise ship for six months; it was one of my first contracts. I travelled to the most wonderful places and saw different cultures and met interesting people. I was so excited I was offered this job, especially, as I was put through a tap audition (I don't tap), but was very experienced at winging it.

We rehearsed in Miami, which was incredible! It was the first time I had ever been abroad and America was my first trip!!! Unfortunately, my fellow cast members weren't such a lovely experience, but a great teaching one. I definitely got a bit of a shock. I put my trust in many of these dancers about personal things I thought they wouldn't share.

I am a bit of a lone ranger. I like my own company and the other dancers found it weird that I would get off at different ports to explore on my own. As usual, anything out of the norm is seen as a bit weird and some people just can't cope with that. They used to make comments in rehearsals about me not executing choreography. The dance captain actually moved me against a wall to tell me that I was walking on thin ice, as well as other threats throughout the contract – when, in fact, I hadn't done anything wrong. She was just down right mean. And I came to the conclusion that I was quite a tough cookie.

I also happened to share a cabin with a girl who locked me out on numerous occasions as she was with her boyfriend. Then, when I invited my mum to come and stay with me, she said, "well, I need my own space," and marched me down to reception to get another room. I don't know why she was so mean!

I also had to get changed in the toilets. They became my dressing area, as there was no room for me in the dressing room. The toilets became my little special place to get changed and, to be honest, it was brilliant!!! I was actually okay there.

The best part of the contract had to be when the dance captain walked on stage with a coat hanger still on her head. It was still on her hat and, to this day, it still makes me smile. Well, that's karma for ya! Don't let anyone get you down!!!

There are a few ways to deal with difficult people that I've found useful over the years:

- Breathe - know that there is nothing anyone can say to hurt you. You have the power to make this choice.
- Always come back with positivity and kindness - people just don't know how to deal with it and it will make you feel good.
- Think if it's worth getting upset about what someone says. Does it really matter?
- Laugh in your mind about the silliness of their comments - you can even give them a funny voice.

- Walk away from negativity and do it in a polite way.

- Don't judge! We don't know why these people act the way they do. Just be thankful you are not one of them.

- If the negativity becomes too much, try to engage in positive conversations and body language.

- Phrase your opinions or suggestions as questions, with a mild tone, so it does not induce an aggressive response from your fellow cast member.

- If all fails and your patience can no longer carry your feet to the next step and your mind feels like it will explode, politely ask for a break and share your worries with someone in charge.

Think of how you would like others to speak to you, or address you, when they feel you are being difficult. You probably would want them to do it respectfully and with kindness. Use that as the benchmark for when you address your concerns with your cast/company members. Be the better person.

• • • • • • • • • • • • •

Casting Couch

As a young woman embarking on my career in the dance industry, I was very trusting, open-hearted, full of passion and was so determined to travel this path with all my heart. So bright-eyed and bushy-tailed, I trusted everyone and everything. I saw no bad in this world, just all the things that were going to come my way and, boy, was I excited!

There are, however, moments that call for vigilance and you learn to trust a little less.

Be aware that there may be times when people may not have your best interests at heart. Just like any other industry, there can be times when we are in situations that don't feel right. Trust your instincts and try to get out of the situation as quickly as possible.

When something feels wrong, it probably is.

Here are the best ways I have dealt with those situations:

- If it feels wrong, then it probably is. Calmly remove yourself from the situation.
- Always leave the situation as politely as you can.

- Try not to get yourself into a difficult situation, know when someone is being genuine, or if they have something else in mind.
- Be vigilant.
- Value yourself.

"Have courage and be kind," Cinderella.

REMEMBER!

- When you are kind to others, the universe will be kind to you, too.
- Always leave the ego in the shower. Without it you can attract, influence and grow closer to people.
- It's a small world; the right attitude could mean less auditions and more referrals over time.
- Trust your instincts, always.
- Learn to calmly and politely extricate yourself out of situations that go against your values.

KNOWLEDGE IS POWER!**

Keep learning and empowering yourself through platforms such as:

- https://www.ted.com/
- http://www.goalcast.com
- http://www.lifescript.com

And if you can find the time, it wouldn't hurt to read the following books:

- *Stronger: Develop The Resilience You Need to Succeed* by Dr George S. Everly, Dr Douglas A. Strouse and Dennis K. McCormack.
- *CHARACTER: Empowering Yourself with Emotional Intelligence (Become Your Best Self Book 1* by Jennifer Freed.

**Website links last checked in January 2017.

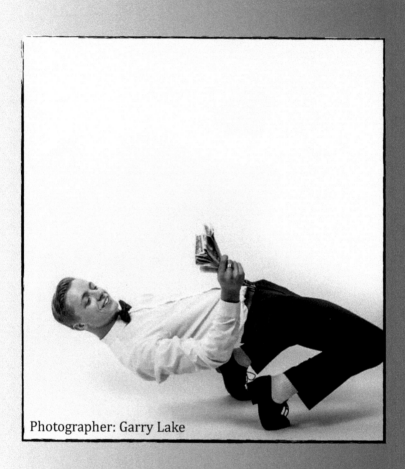

Photographer: Garry Lake

Chapter 9

How to Survive When Out of Work

(Disclaimer: I am not a registered or accredited financial advisor. My advice is based on my personal experiences.)

Many students and dancers have asked me how they could survive financially when out of work, so below are some suggestions of what seem to work best for performers.

• • • • • • • • • • • • •

Part-Time Work

So what do you do when you are not treading the boards? For most of us, this means a part-time job to pay the bills.

One of the largest areas I find performers start to lose their focus is when they take on work that exhausts them so much they don't have the energy to audition. Sadly, many performers get used to the money they are making and can often, all too easily, forget about their goals. All of this is very common and you'll find performers giving up before they've even started.

The best way to avoid this is to try to do something that involves the arts, so it can be a constant reminder that you are still working towards your goal. Here are my few suggestions for part-time work for you to consider and their advantages:

F.O.H (Front of House) Staff

Front of House is a wonderful way to stay connected with the industry. You will be surrounded by all the benefits of live theatre, whilst being paid. Your motivation will be at an all-time high when you see the performances on stage reminding you just how close you are to being on that stage yourself.

Benefits:

- The magic of theatre will motivate you.
- Meeting actors, choreographers, and directors.
- A different perspective of theatre, helping you to understand your craft more.
- Opportunity to work on your networking skills.
- Opportunity to be surrounded by like-minded people.
- Flexible hours.

Dance Studio Receptionist / Dance Agencies

It's a wonderful way to still stay involved and in shape as you will be surrounded by choreographers, teachers, and dancers. You will have the first word on upcoming castings and auditions, some of which you may be able to attend. You won't have to travel far for classes, they will be right on your doorstep, so you are more likely to take part. Being surrounded by dancers that are improving and maintaining skills will only serve to motivate you to do the same.

Ask around at places that offer dance classes, and take your CV in person - face value always works better. Look at studios in your local area or, if you are in London, you have Pineapple Dance Studios, Dance Attic, Danceworks, etc. Please look at Chapter 4 where I talk about classes.

Benefits:

- Reduced class fees or maybe even free classes.
- Meeting and being surrounded by people within the industry.
- Constant and direct contact with casting directors, producers, choreographers, etc.
- Use of studio space.
- Flexible hours.
- Maintaining technique and stamina.
- Learn new styles of dance.

Using websites such as https://www.onedanceuk.org you can find a list of different agencies/ studios to reach out to.

Teaching

Teaching your craft has many benefits. Not only are you increasingly becoming more familiar with the ever-evolving dance scene, you are also working on your own technique by breaking down movement and demonstrating it. I found when I started to teach, there were a lot of elements I found hard to explain, but when I looked at it in detail, it actually helped me with my own technique. I have now nailed the execution of my pirouettes, am strong and have not lost any flexibility in all these years due to teaching. It's a great way to keep you on top of your game and get paid for it!!!

There are a lot of dance schools out there looking for young people to bring in new energy. Many people are seeing the many health benefits of dance, so dance teachers will always be needed. It's also a great confidence builder.

Why not start up your own classes? You could look at village halls or places to rent within your area. Dance is huge and there are a lot of people that want to improve their fitness as well as have fun.

Benefits:
- Ability to work on your technique as well as help those whom you are teaching.
- Stamina enhancement.
- Increased knowledge of your craft.
- Skills development, as they evolve and grow.
- Ability to increase creative skills as you create new choreography for your students. This is also how I got into choreography.
- Having the outlet of dancing. We need it!

- Working with like-minded people who understand your goals.
- Working with other dancers and choreographers who may have upcoming projects.
- You are still surrounded by your industry and this will be a reminder that you are still in the game and working towards your goal.

Where to find teaching jobs:
- Mandy Network, www.mandy.com
- The Stage, www.thestage.co.uk
- Facebook – The Hustle, https://www.facebook.com/groups/HustleCommunity/
- Dance Teacher Network UK, http://www.dancenetworkassociation.org.uk/dance-teachers-network-

Promotional Work

Promotional work is great!! It's very flexible and there are a lot of performers on the books of promotional agents, so they know and understand about auditions and the time needed off.

Promotional work also pays well and it's not going to exhaust you. Again, you will be working with like-minded people. Performers may have information on upcoming castings and auditions. Also, the simple fact that you can talk to people that have an understanding of your industry, you are not going to feel so alone - this can only be a good thing.

Benefits:

- Very flexible.
- Good pay rates.
- Opportunity to work on your networking skills.
- Opportunity to be surrounded by like - minded people.
- Won't be physically or mentally draining.
- Get a few freebies.

Below are a few promotional companies that you could reach out to for work:

- Breeze People, http://www.breezepeople.co.uk
- Push, http://pushpromotions.co.uk
- Hel's Angels, http://www.helsangels.net/staff-hub/
- Varii, http://www.varii-promotions.co.uk
- Kreate, http://www.kreate.co.uk
- Stuck For Staff, http://stuckforstaff.co.uk/
- Yes People, http://www.yespeople.co.uk
- Lola Staffing, http://www.temptribe.co.uk

- Mash Staffing Specialists, http://www.mashstaffing.com/uk/
- Elite, http://www.elitepromo.co.uk

Just like everything else in life, it is better to go with reputable and registered companies as opposed to taking on dance jobs that sound too good to be true.

Singing For Your Supper

This is a great way to not only improve and work on your singing skills, but you could also get recognised, as you never know who may come in. There are a number of ways you can enter this line of work. There are companies such as The Singing Waiters, who secretly place singers amongst a crowd of people. But, you could also go through entertainment agencies. However, there are a lot of bands, duo's, etc. so you really need to make sure that you are in contact with the agencies you sign up with, otherwise you may get lost in a sea of acts, should you decide to go down this route.

Benefits:

- Working and developing singing skills.
- Exposing vocal skills.
- Working on performance skills.
- Interaction with industry professionals.
- Building confidence.
- Building singing repertoire.
- Flexible hours.
- Pays well.

Here is a list of companies and agencies:

- www.thethreewaiters.co.uk
- www.singing-waiters.co.uk
- www.secretsingers.com
- www.singerspro.com
- www.mandy.com

As mentioned above with Promotional Work, it is better to go with reputable and registered companies, as opposed to taking on dance jobs that sound too good to be true.

· · · · · · · · · · · · · ·

Making Your Money Make Sense

Dancing is beautiful. Without a good grasp on your finances, the mental and emotional stress from this aspect of being self-employed could take away the beauty of what you love to do.

To get on top of your finances, you have to live within your means first. What does living within your means look like? Budgeting is at the core of it, but to get there, let's look at the key questions you need to be asking yourself where your money is concerned:

Sit down and look at your bank statements. What's your cash flow looking like? Do you know where all your income is coming from? Are you happy with all the sources or would you like to increase your income? What are you spending your money on? Is it realistic spending that leaves you with money in the bank at the end of the month or does it leave you in the red?

 If you are constantly in the red at the end of every month and can't seem to tell exactly where your money is going, don't get overwhelmed. Start tracking your expenses. You could do it the easy way, where you withdraw cash on a weekly basis and record everything you buy in Excel or your notebook as a way to figure out your spending patterns.

Manually tracking expenses can be daunting. Thankfully, there are Apps that you can use for that and save you the stress. An example is GoodBudget Budget Planner: Money and Expense Tracker, which, is available on both Android and iOS stores.

There are also blogs by people from different industries that share their financial journeys - what they are struggling with, how they are moving forward, etc. These are great, as they create a sense of community around people trying to achieve the same goal (choose one that resonates with you). Some I have found useful include:

- Finance Girl, http://www.financegirl.co.uk
- Martin Lewis' Blog,
  http://blog.moneysavingexpert.com
- Savvy Scott, http://savvyscot.com
- You Could Save, http://www.youcouldsave.co.uk
- Miss Thrifty, http://www.miss-thrifty.co.uk

· · · · · · · · · · · · · ·

How Long Do You Hold Out For That Job?

In our careers as dancers, most of us will go through a time when we have to make a decision about how long we will wait for a job before taking others which, although good jobs, aren't our ultimate dream.

For example, say you have been offered a contract that starts in November - they auditioned early or they have asked you back from last year. They want you to sign in July!!! This will mean that between signing and starting, you have been given four months, so you can't go for that year contract in a musical or that tour you would like to do. What do you do then?

If you don't take the contract that's offered to you, what if you get nothing and then, to put the icing on the cake, you don't even get the contract offered in July?

This is a dilemma you may come across a few times.

My advice - although simple and maybe cliché - close your eyes, take a deep breath, and go with your gut instinct. I believe that if you don't want to cut yourself off from doing what you really want, then don't stop yourself, just do it!

You have come this far, you have worked this hard and, yes, the contract you were offered will give you the chance to perform, but would you be as happy as you would dancing in that tour or in the West End? You can find other work while waiting, as mentioned at the beginning of this chapter, and stay motivated by reading the beginning of this book.

If you have an agent and you have a good relationship with them, then talk to them and evaluate what they say. But, above all, go with your gut - it will almost always point you in the right direction.

. . . .

When A Job Falls Through

When I was about 22, I was sent to an audition for a new movie that was coming out. It sounded awesome and there were big names in the movie. I arrived at the audition and there was definitely an element of excitement in the air. The dancers looked tentative and I could see them all thinking, "what if, what if".

The audition was very jazzy and, at that time in my life, I loved jazz! It was my favourite and I absolutely loved the audition. We were taught about three sections and the choreographer made cuts throughout.

Eeek, I was still there.

I felt really comfortable in this audition - like it was almost choreographed for me. I loved the style, loved the choreographer and the whole experience was just wonderful!

As we finished the last section, the choreographer looked at the people who had made it until the end. There were probably about 15 of us left. She needed five. She went around the circle and picked two people. Then she looked at me and pointed.

OMG are you kidding me! I wanted to throw my arms around her, ring my mum and celebrate. However, I calmly walked next to the other dancers and waited there till she had picked the other two. I was on the verge of shaking, I was so excited.

Brilliant, I could finally give some good news to my family!

Once the audition finished, there was no waiting around. We were driven to the studios in a lovely car and our measurements were taken for the costumes. We were to start rehearsing the following week.

This was all too exciting and the day was my best one yet.

We arrived at the studios, the sun was shining beautifully in London. Sometimes London can feel like a lonely place, when you don't know anyone and you are fighting to achieve your dream. However, I had never seen London look as beautiful as it did that day; everything was just like I dreamed. Our measurements were taken, we were thanked and then we were free to go. It was a Friday and we were due to start rehearsing the following week. They were going to contact my agent, so there was only one thing to do: celebrate! I rang my mum, my nan, and my dog!

That night I decided to celebrate with my boyfriend at the time. Why not? I had worked so hard for this. This was the stuff that dreams were made of! I had a great night and was on top of the world.

So, on the Monday morning I rang my agent to make sure they had all the information and they knew I had secured the job. I was so happy to ring them with such good news.

"Hi, it's Taira!" (Obviously very excited to tell them the news).
"Hi, Taira." (they seemed quite subdued).
"I am ringing to say that I got that job you sent me for - you know the movie? And I would like to know my schedule please."
"Well, erm, I am really sorry, but they contacted us this morning to say they have replaced your character with a man."

Pause. Stop. Everything stopped. Nothing made sense. My stomach felt empty and I wanted to cry.

"What! Really? How could this be? No! No! This can't happen! I can't ring my parents and tell them once again it didn't work out! Oh, please, don't make me do that!"

"Okay", I replied. There was nothing I could do, I knew this, but it didn't make it any easier.

They said they were really sorry. I needed to sit down and had never felt so low. I started to think it would be better if I were never offered the job at all than being put through this.

Why didn't they like me? What had I done wrong? Should I not have celebrated? Was it karma? Was it my fault? I had so many questions!

Whatever it was, it hurt like hell and left me feeling deflated. How much more would I have to take until I could just get a job and perform? That's all I wanted to do! Do what I love! Do what I was supposed to!

After a couple of hours, I had to make the calls to my family to tell them it didn't quite work out. This was another massive ache in my stomach, knowing I would have to go through this again.

Aghhhhhhh, why me? Why not someone else?

In this business, there are going to be times when jobs fall through. This could be due to funding issues, producers not having enough money, low ticket sales, shows being pulled, and even shows that you have started rehearsing for. There are many reasons and, unfortunately, you may have to go through the process of getting the job only to have it taken away from you.

It will feel like the end of the world for some of you, as it did for me. You must try to rise above it. See it as a moment to build on your strength and move on. I guess it's easy for me to say that now, but I know how I felt then and I got through it. So can you!

Yes, it's shit! Yes, you will feel like rubbish and, yes, you will make it to the other side. Trust me.

There is something else waiting for you, something wonderful, just keep going.

· · · · · · · · · · · · ·

Retirement and Tax Assessments

When it comes to your retirement, there are three basic pension funds. The first is a pension fund that both you and your employer contribute to. The second pension fund is a personal one. You have to contribute to this yourself on a monthly basis to ensure that when you finally retire you aren't living off other people's scraps. The last pension is the Basic State Pension, which you get when you reach retirement age. Realistically, it isn't a lot of money.

You have to think about your future, investigate all the above and see what will work for you. You are young and can work now and retirement seems so far away, but don't dismiss it and make sure you plan ahead.

The Equity Members' Personal Pension Scheme is the only one into which theatre, radio and TV employers pay. Members need to register (free) to take out an individual policy, so you can give the number to employers.

- Pensions Advisory Service, 0300 123 1047
  http://www.pensionsadvisoryservice.org.uk

• • • • • • • • • • • • •

Tax: Self-Assessment For Dancers

We all dread the beginning of the year, as we know we have to do our self- assessment tax returns. This is because, in the UK, dancers are always considered self-employed. Please look at this link, as it will help you understand how it all works and if you need to register:

- www.**dancers**info.co.uk/tax-awareness/employed-or-**self**-employed/

• •

"Go confidently in the direction of your dreams!
Live the life you imagined," Thoreau.

REMEMBER!

- Live within your means.
- Part-time work is to help you take your career to the next level, never to give up on it!
- It helps to always prepare for the worst, but expect the best out of life, financially.

KNOWLEDGE IS POWER!**

Keep learning and empowering yourself through platforms such as:

- http://www.thisismoney.co.uk/money/saving/index.html
- http://www.practicalmoneyskills.com
- https://www.moneyadviceservice.org.uk/en
- http://www.pensionsadvisoryservice.org.uk

And if you can find the time, it wouldn't hurt to read the following books:

- *The 9 Steps to Financial Freedom* by Suze Orman.
- *Think and Grow Rich* by Napoleon Hill.
- *The Courage to Be Rich* by Suze Orman.

**Website links last checked in January 2017.

Photographer: Rolfe Klement

Chapter 10

Beyond Dancing

As a dancer, we are told it's a very short-lived career, but I disagree. There are so many more pathways after performing; some of you may even go onto performing well into your late 40s, if you are lucky. I have a lot of friends that are doing the same, so why not you? It also doesn't have to be the end of your career if you do decide to stop performing. You might end up staying in the industry in one role or another, or you could end up in a completely different industry. The choice is yours.

The Casting Director, Irene Cotton, comments, "apart from my work as a Casting Director for theatre, film, tv and musical theatre, I do a number of workshops and talks about how to sustain a career in this extremely difficult profession. As I started my working life as a dancer, I am aware of the difficulties, along with the joys, of that world, so feel I am qualified to also talk to dancers. I think that the more skills you have, alongside your main talent, i.e. drama or dance, the more you are likely to survive and have a lifetime's career. For dancers, when time allows, have singing lesson and drama lessons; if you play an instrument, even solely at school level, keep that up as well. These are all skills which can be used to get you work during your dance career or after it has ended. Many dancers now work in shows where acting and singing are required and there are many productions now for actor/musicians/dancers. This is a viewpoint which is now held by most Casting Directors and Directors in our business and I know it helps performers to sustain a successful career for many years."

There are a few major points I want to cover about life beyond dancing, but, really, this is a much larger issue. One that requires, I feel, more attention and, therefore, I am currently writing a book on what lies beyond a dance career and how to prepare for it. I've realised that dance really does become, for many dancers, their identity. And when that identity has been taken away, when the routine no longer exists, some people are left despondent with no sense of direction. Anxiety and depression could easily follow, if we can't see the avenues and the next stages available to us.

We've put our all into our training and career, taken hours and hours of technique classes and been through the greatest highs and the lowest of lows. And some of you have already dedicated most of your lives to this profession.

So how do you make the switch? How do we begin something again when we have given so much to our craft?

Your skills in dance are much more transferable than you think. Use the discipline from your art - dedication, focus, vision and drive - to follow your dreams. Think of all those skills you can pass on through teaching, coaching and inspiring others to do exactly what you have done.

Wellness is one of the biggest industries now and guess what? Dance is considered a part of that. There will always be a demand for dance in one way or the other and the great thing about it is you can choose the format. If you still want to perform, how about acting, musical theatre character parts or physical theatre companies? The great thing about performing in your 40s is there are fewer people doing it than those in their 20s.

I never thought I could be as happy creating and teaching as I did when I was on the stage. I absolutely do now and you, too, can get that same feeling. If you are creative then why not move into choreographing or directing? This is also a hard profession, but one that you have built resilience for with your years of training and auditioning, so why not?

You might also be interested in working behind the scenes in production, stage management, or company management. The list is endless. I have listed a few ideas below that I think may help you understand the vastness of what you can do after you finish performing. There's a beautiful life beyond dance. You just have to position yourself for it.

· · · · · · · · · · · · ·

STAYING IN THE INDUSTRY

Here are opportunities that your training and experience could be right for:

- Creative Directing
- Choreographer
- Movement Director
- Theatre Director
- Film Maker
- Music Editing/Producing
- Starting your own performance company

Production

- Stage Management
- ASM
- DSM
- Company Manger
- Sound Designer
- Lighting Designer

Teaching

- Primary Schools
- Secondary Schools
- Vocational Schools
- Private Schools

- Universities
- Stage Schools
- Youth Theatre Companies
- Community
- Start your own school

Performance

- Acting
- TV Extra Work
- Musical Theatre / Character Roles
- Physical Theatre
- Singing Career

Agencies

- Musical Theatre
- Dance
- Acting
- Film and TV
- Entertainment Agencies
- Create your own agency

Health and Wellness Industry

- Yoga
- Pilates
- Masseur

- Nutritionist

Dance Organisations

- Dance Agencies across the UK
- Arts Council of England
- Equity
- Outreach

Dance Companies

- Administrative roles
- Managing positions
- Daily company operations

Put the same passion into a new position that you put into your dance and you will find your way.

• • • • • • • • • • • • • •

Roles Outside of Dance

There are a lot of wonderful opportunities that have absolutely nothing to do with dance out there. You are capable of anything you put your mind to. Don't see it as giving up. You may feel you are going to disappoint family and loved ones around you because they have supported you and you are letting them down, but this simply isn't the case. I think those who are brave enough to admit that they want a new direction in life are very admirable. It's a brave move to admit this and, at the end of the day, it's your life and your happiness. So, choose what's right for you.

So, when you are done with dance, what do you love that you can see yourself doing for a very long time?

Now that you know what you would like to do, what's next? You have to find out the qualification(s) needed to get through the door of your next best job. There are, of course, careers that will require you to study full time, should you have the time and money to do so. Search for the qualification you would like to pursue from over 700 universities and colleges in the UK on http://www.thecompleteuniversityguide.co.uk/distance-learning.

Whilst all these possibilities - getting an education, staying in the industry or basic employment skills might seem easier to some, to others they might be scary. Not to worry, there's a place where you can find guidance and help. Dancers' Career Development (DCD), http://www.thedcd.org.uk/index.php, can help you with mentoring, training and how to access grants, as you transition from dance to another career. One Dance UK is another organisation that offers a mentoring scheme each year for mid-career dance artists - www.onedanceuk.org/careers/professionaldevelopment/.../dancers-mentoring/.

. . . .

Developing Your Skills Through Dance

The technological innovations that we continue to see everyday mean that the future workplace is going to be very different to what it is today. Beyond getting a qualification, there are skills that you can develop during your dance career - the same skills that even non-dancers also have to learn.

Some of these skills you could develop and master through the content of this guide and some of the reading material suggested. Future employers are looking for people that communicate well and know how to present information with clarity. If you go back to Chapter 2 on how to brand yourself, you will realise that by applying some of the content, these skills become a part of your everyday life.

Interpersonal relationships' management and leadership skills should be something you are likely to master from all the different dance situations you are thrown into. Your exposure to the world through dance travel, meeting and engaging dancers from different backgrounds and working with them without ego, helping each other along and most importantly encouraging others, are all part of those skills.

Critical thinking skills, which refer to the ability to make clear decisions and solve problems, you learn throughout your dance career on an almost daily basis. You can, however, enhance them through simple things like puzzles, crosswords, reading material out of your comfort zone, and conditioning yourself to always look for solutions to challenges you or your loved ones face. The more problems you solve, the easier it will become for this to become second nature to you - that's what employers want, even if you have limited experience in your new career.

IT skills require you to know the basics of using most of the technology you already have at your fingertips. If you can use your mobile to send texts or emails, surely you would know how to do the same on a computer or laptop? If not, then learn.

If you struggle with grammar or how to write your thoughts effectively and succinctly, then look up free courses online to help you with this. There are a lot of platforms to learn from. You just have to Google them. Did you know you can find numerous manuals for free online about how to learn simple applications like Word, Excel, and PowerPoint? You can find them as either text documents or videos on YouTube.

To learn university level material, you can use the likes of Coursera, https://www.coursera.org for free.

And here's a link to what you can do with a performing arts degree - https://www.prospects.ac.uk/careers-advice/what...i.../performing-arts-dance-drama

Feel inspired by what others had to say about their lives beyond dance here - http://www.roh.org.uk/news/life-after-dance-why-hanging-up-dancing-shoes-neednt-be-the-end-of-a-career

· ·

"A wise man adapts himself to circumstance, as water shapes itself to the vessel that contains it,"

Chinese Proverb.

REMEMBER!

- There's life beyond dancing.
- Preparation is the key to success.
- Knowledge is power. The more you know about how to get what you want, the less stressed your journey will be.

KNOWLEDGE IS POWER!**

Keep learning and empowering yourself through platforms such as:

- http://www.thedcd.org.uk/index.php
- https://www.livecareer.com/quintessential

And if you can find the time, it wouldn't hurt to read the following books:

- *Making Changes – Facilitating The Transition of Dancers to Post – Performance Careers.* Research Report by William J. Baumol, Joan Jeffri, and David Throsby, www.cpanda.org/data/a00191/changes.pdf
- *The Career Change Handbook* by Graham Green.
- *Strategies for Career Change: Finding Your Very Best Next Work Life* by Martha E. Mangelsdorf.

**Website links last checked in January 2017.

Epilogue

Dance Has Brought Me Here

Yesterday I was walking through London. The sun was shining and the weather was beautiful. I was on my way to meeting a couple of producers as a choreographer - my next adventure.

As I walked over the Embankment, I suddenly realised that everywhere I have been was because I chose to follow my instinct and passion. I chose to dance! I have met many different people and some have become friends and some acquaintances. I have learned from them and had experiences with them because of dance. I am walking in the sunshine in London because dance has brought me here. And it's wonderful!

There is so much more to dance than a paso doble, a pirouette or a split leap. If you have chosen to follow your career in dance because you feel it is your purpose, then that has huge merit and it is a step towards a happier life. You might not be the richest person, but you will be wealthy in the happiness that comes from choosing what you love.

You have every right to be in this industry - only you can make this work. I hope you take the steps you need to take and embrace the great times with the not so good. Meet wonderful people and travel the world! This career could take you anywhere in the world, but you must allow yourself to enjoy it. Become stronger!

Develop as a performer and as a human! Love and live every minute.

If you feel like you need a bit of motivation on the days that are slower than others, I hope you can use this book as a guide, a friend and someone that believes in you.

Your world awaits...

Lots of love,

T x

· ·

Bibliography

Abdul, P. (n.d.). AZQuotes.com. Retrieved July 19, 2017, from AZQuotes.com Web site: *http://www.azquotes.com/quote/475*

Anderson, E. (2017). *Teenagers spend 27 hours a week online: how internet use has ballooned in the last decade.* [online] Telegraph.co.uk. Available at: *http://www.telegraph.co.uk/finance/ newsbysector/mediatechnologyandtelecoms/digital-media/ 11597743/Teenagers-spend-27-hours-a-week-online-how-internet-use-has-ballooned-in-the-last-decade.html* [Accessed 11 Jul 2017].

Confucius. (n.d.). AZQuotes.com. Retrieved July 19, 2017, from AZQuotes.com Web site: *http://www.azquotes.com/quote/510953*

Ford, H. (1947). *The Reader's Digest*, Volume 51, (Filler item), Quote Page 64, The Reader's Digest Association. (Verified on paper).

Frankel, B. and Adamson, E. (2014). *Naturally thin*. New York: Touchstone.

Graham, M. (n.d.). AZQuotes.com. Retrieved July 19, 2017, from AZQuotes.com Web site: http://www.azquotes.com/quote/ 521803

Head, E. (n.d.). AZQuotes.com. Retrieved July 19, 2017, from AZQuotes.com Web site: *http://www.azquotes.com/quote/127878*

Jackson, M. (1987). Interview with Michael Jackson. Interview by Darryl Dennard for *Ebony/Jet Magazine,* 13 Nov.

Jackson.M , Available at *http://www.azquotes.com/quote/1344396* {Accessed 26/06/2017}

Larson, C. (n.d.). AZQuotes.com. Retrieved July 19, 2017, from AZQuotes.com Web site: *http://www.azquotes.com/quote/397197*

Mandela, N. (n.d.). AZQuotes.com. Retrieved July 20, 2017, from AZQuotes.com Web site: *http://www.azquotes.com/quote/185315*

Pavlova, A. (n.d.). AZQuotes.com. Retrieved July 19, 2017, from AZQuotes.com Web site: *http://www.azquotes.com/quote/521847*

Thoreau, H. (n.d.). AZQuotes.com. Retrieved July 19, 2017, from AZQuotes.com Web site: *http://www.azquotes.com/quote/415176*

Warner, K. (2015). '"Jem and the Holograms" Star Aubrey Peeples: "Don't Worry What You Look Like as Long as You're Healthy"', *Cosmopolitan,* 23 Oct 2015. Available at: *http://www.cosmopolitan.com/entertainment/movies/q-and-a/a48142/jem-and-the-holograms-aubrey-peeples-interview/* [Accessed 19 Jul 2017].

Wehr, J. (1945). *Cinderella*. New York, Stephen Daye.

Winfrey, O. (2003). *What I Know for Sure*. [online] *oprah.com*. Available at: *http://www.oprah.com/omagazine/what-i-know-for-sure-hard-work* [Accessed 19 Jul 2017].